ANIMAL QUILTS

ANIMAL QUILTS

12 Paper Piecing Patterns for
Stunning Animal Quilt Designs

Juliet van der Heijden

DAVID & CHARLES

www.davidandcharles.com

CONTENTS

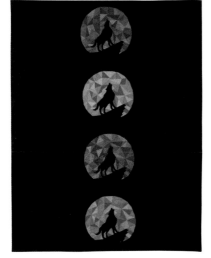

INTRODUCTION

I grew up in Edinburgh, but much of my childhood was spent enjoying the magnificent countryside of the Scottish Highlands. We would go for long hill walks, wade through rivers, pick wild berries and marvel at the heathers and wild flowers. My family spent what felt like an eternity birdwatching, peering through their binoculars in search of golden eagles, short-eared owls, buzzards, ospreys and all sorts of other amazing birds. Now, I must admit that as the youngest member of the family, I didn't always have the best attention span for birdwatching, but those hours spent enjoying nature left their mark on me. Although I didn't appreciate it at the time, they ingrained me with a deep-seated love of the outdoors and the wonders that can be found there.

Try as I might, I could never capture the beauty of birds and animals with pencil or paints, so it was a great joy to find my artistic canvas in quilting, and more specifically in foundation paper piecing. I discovered that the mix of creativity and logic involved in designing paper-pieced patterns suits my skills perfectly. It never fails to amaze me when I see the complex shapes that can be created just by sewing a series of straight lines. I can't resist the challenge of creating patterns which may appear complicated, but once the basics of the technique have been mastered, only require the sewer to be able to count and sew a straight line. Experience has taught me that a small change to the constructions of a pattern can make a huge difference to the ease with which it can be sewn. As such, I pieced all of the quilts in this book multiple times and tweaked the patterns until I was happy that they were constructed in the most logical way possible. My very first pattern was a butterfly and I quickly went on to discover a love of depicting animals and birds in fabric. It became a challenge to create creatures in my designs that had personality and jumped out of the fabric. I didn't want my designs to be lifeless and static.

The patterns in this book depict birds and animals from all over the world. I started the book with plans to limit myself to a specific region or species of birds or animals, but in the end I settled for no themes, no rules – just the creation of the best possible set of quilts. Some are the result of very personal inspiration, others were designed for my family or as the result of a random spark of inspiration.

As I designed more and more patterns, I began to feel limited by traditional 12in blocks. The small size didn't allow me to add the amount of detail that I wanted and it restricted the types of fabrics I could use. By increasing the size, I discovered that I could make the patterns more elaborate and, excitingly, I could also be more adventurous with fabric. The smallest quilt design in this book is 21in x 14in, the biggest is 50in x 50in, with a wide variety of sizes in between. The designs can be used to create mini quilts, cushions, play quilts for babies, lap quilts and bed-size quilts. You can sew a single animal or sew multiple versions and combine them in a single quilt. The possibilities are both endless and exciting.

USING THIS BOOK

People often ask whether my patterns are suitable for beginners. It's a difficult question to answer as paper piecing can be a challenging technique for some people to learn, while others pick it up quickly and without problems. In general, I would suggest that it is probably better to learn the technique on simpler patterns than the ones in this book, but if you are an adventurous beginner, please don't let this put you off. I have tried to provide you with all the guidance you will need, but it is important that you read the early chapters on my foundation piecing method.

The Getting Started section of the book looks at issues directly related to paper piecing. Topics such as equipment you will need, how to paper piece, perfecting your technique and fabric choices are covered in depth.

The Projects section looks at the individual patterns. Instructions are given on the construction of the blocks as well as how to complete each quilt. Within each chapter there are two main diagrams provided to assist you (these are not to scale). A Colour Diagram of the project gives an overview of the sections that need to be pieced together and is a great reference when deciding which colour each individual piece should be. A Colouring Chart allows you to experiment with fabric colour choices and try out your ideas before committing them to fabric. These two diagrams are shown reversed, as foundation piecing is worked from the back of the printed design.

Within the General Techniques section, instructions are given on more general quilting techniques, such as adding borders, sewing binding and creating cushions. As such, this book talks you through every stage of the quilt-making process.

The patterns in this book vary in difficulty. Many of them contain a lot of fabric pieces, but are relatively straightforward to sew. Others need careful attention to detail when the paper sections are sewn together so that the outlines do not have 'bites' taken out of them. In general, the larger the pattern pieces, the harder a pattern is to sew, especially when the fabric pieces on these sections vary greatly in size. Many quilters are almost as wary of Y-seams as they are of paper piecing. I can put their minds at rest – none of my patterns have Y-seams.

DOWNLOADING THE PATTERNS

Go to www.davidandcharles.com to download the files containing the following:

- The Paper Pattern Templates for all the projects in the book. Please note that there are two different pages for each pattern. In order to minimize printing issues, one version has been formatted specifically for A4 paper, while the other has been formatted specifically for Letter paper.

- Pattern Assembly Diagrams. These diagrams show how the templates are distributed on the page and will provide reference when gluing templates together.

- Colour Diagrams.

- Colouring Charts. This diagram has two equally important purposes. For those wanting to try out different colour combinations, it can be printed and coloured in to help with fabric choices. For those with young children, the Colouring Chart can serve as a welcome distraction while Mum sneaks a few precious moments of quilting time!

- Number Diagrams. These place the pattern pieces within the context of the pattern as a whole. Although these diagrams can be printed out, I would suggest that they are best viewed on a computer screen where it is possible to zoom in and out and study all the relevant details. Some people may prefer to use this diagram as the Colouring Chart to as to keep all information together in one place, the choice is yours.

- Quilt Assembly Diagrams. These diagrams have only been provided for those quilts in the book that require borders and the combination of more than one block.

Please note that templates and diagrams have been provided for *all* blocks sewn in this book. As such, where mirror image blocks are required for a quilt, you will find all the relevant patterns for both a right-facing block and a left-facing block.

GETTING STARTED

EQUIPMENT

This section describes my workspace and the equipment that I use when creating my paper-pieced quilts.

SETTING UP YOUR WORKSPACE

When paper piecing, it helps to have your workspace set up in a logical way. There are three things that you will be doing a lot – cutting, sewing and pressing. As such, you will need easy access to a cutting mat, a sewing machine and an ironing board. I set my sewing machine in front of me. I am right-handed, so I place my cutting board directly beside me on my right side and the ironing board on my left side. I sit on a desk chair with wheels and scoot between the three areas. Set the ironing board up at the same height as your sewing machine, so that you can comfortably iron while sitting down. This has the added advantage that the ironing board can act as an extension of your sewing table and can support large paper templates when necessary. It is important to have good light when paper piecing. A room with natural light is helpful, but I also have a bright table lamp directly next to my sewing machine, which can be used at all times.

ESSENTIAL EQUIPMENT

The good news is that you don't need to have too much fancy equipment to be able to paper piece. Here is a list of the basic kit that you will need.

- Sewing machine

- Iron and ironing board

- Rotary cutter and cutting mat (although it is possible to work purely with fabric scissors if you prefer)

- Quilting ruler

- Paper for printing patterns

- Paper scissors

- Paper glue (if you are sewing a large pattern)

- Pins (not plastic-headed pins as these can melt when ironed)

- Quick unpick/seam ripper (hopefully you won't need this, but better safe than sorry!)

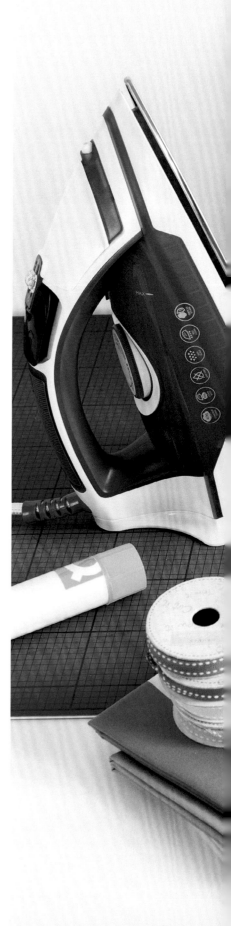

ADDITIONAL EQUIPMENT

While it is true that you can paper piece without too much fancy equipment, there are definitely a few tools that can make life easier.

Add-A-Quarter Ruler™

The Add-A-Quarter ruler is a simple ruler with a ¼in lip running along the edge. It allows you to butt the ¼in lip up against the folded paper when trimming seams and to cut a perfect ¼in seam every time with no danger of the ruler slipping. When I first purchased this ruler, I was determined not to like it. I thought it was a gimmick and was cynical as to whether it was really needed, but over time I found myself reaching past my standard quilting ruler in search of it. I am now a true convert and love using it.

Light Box

A light box is still on my list of items to buy. Although I have limited experience of using them myself, I have taught classes where there have been light boxes present. In general, those using light boxes have got to grips with the technique faster and more easily than those holding their fabric up to the light.

Walking Foot

I strongly recommend using a walking foot when sewing together the individual paper foundations of a pattern. The bigger the pattern, the more helpful the walking foot is, as it stops the sewing machine from slipping on the paper and keeps everything lined up correctly.

Plastic Clips

Clover Wonder Clips can be really helpful when sewing paper foundations together, as they can be used to clip pieces of paper together.

Paper

Opinions are split as to what type of paper you should use when foundation paper piecing. I must admit that due to the volume of paper piecing that I do and the large size of many of these patterns, I generally tend to stick to normal 80gsm-weight printer paper. It has the advantages of being cheap and easily available. The disadvantage of printer paper is that it is not as easy to see through as vellum and paper specifically designed for paper piecing. It is also sturdier and as such harder to remove at the end.

Thread

I have recently started piecing using 80-weight thread. This is a really fine thread that leads to the stitches becoming virtually invisible. An advantage of 80-weight thread is that it doesn't add extra bulk to seams. As layers of fabric can easily build up in the seam allowances of paper-pieced patterns, it is great not to have thread compounding the problem. I was initially worried that 80-weight thread would be too thin and would break, but I have not had a single thread break when removing papers, and I have deliberately pulled some of the papers off quite roughly to test the thread strength. I tend to use light grey or ecru thread as these shades are neutral and blend into most fabrics.

Needles

I tend to use 80/12 size machine needles for paper piecing, but at times, when I am using more delicate fabrics, such as Liberty and Oakshott cottons, I will switch to a thinner 70/11 needle.

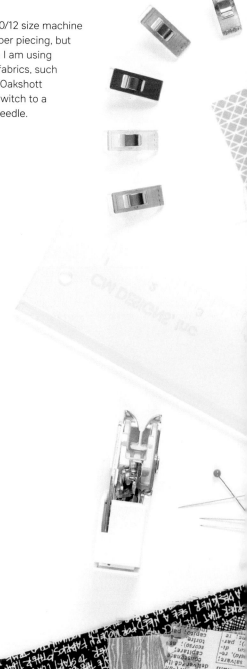

PAPER PIECING

There are two types of paper piecing – English paper piecing and foundation paper piecing – but they are very different techniques. English paper piecing is done by wrapping the fabric around paper templates and then using tiny hand stitches to sew the individual templates together. The templates can be removed intact at the end of a project and reused many times. Foundation paper piecing is where fabric is sewn directly onto a paper foundation. The stitching is done on a sewing machine using tiny stitches that perforate and weaken the paper. When the sewing is complete, the paper is peeled away, leaving a beautiful piece of patchwork. Each time that you sew a foundation paper-pieced pattern you need a new paper foundation, as the original one is destroyed in the sewing process.

I work purely with foundation paper piecing. Any time that I mention paper piecing in this book, it is specifically foundation paper piecing that I am referring to. Although some foundation paper-pieced patterns will work for English paper piecing, I am pretty sure that the patterns in this book will not. There are too many tiny pieces that would be awkward for English paper piecing.

In both forms of paper piecing, the paper is there to provide stability. It stops fabric from warping (even when sewn on the bias). The paper also allows pieces to be sewn that are considerably smaller and more awkwardly shaped than would normally be considered in quilting.

PAPER PIECING PERSONALITY

When I first started quilting, I was at a stage in my life when I needed a challenge. I noticed that people around me shuddered with fear at the mention of foundation paper piecing and decided that it sounded like the perfect challenge for me.

I'm not going to lie, there was frustration in the early days, but as I developed a methodology that worked for me I also gained a fascination for the technique. I discovered that there are many different ways to foundation paper piece and that the reason so many people dislike paper piecing is that they have not found a piecing technique that suits their personality. The method that I describe in this book works for me, but I am realistic enough to

acknowledge that it may not work for everyone. If you find that you are making mistake after mistake, then the chances are that a different technique would work better for you. That's absolutely ok with me. Go and search the internet for tutorials and keep trying. I would prefer that you try somebody else's technique than give up on paper piecing completely. We all have different strengths and weaknesses and our brains work in different ways. Some people love to be as precise as they possibly can be and to minimize fabric wastage by accurately pre-cutting all their fabric. Other people prefer to save their sanity and cut their fabric a bit more generously. Neither of these methods is right or wrong – they just work better for some people than for others. Even if you are an experienced paper piecer, I suggest that you read through the method section of the book as you may be able to pick up a few tips. Sometimes one or two small tweaks to your technique can make all the difference to your enjoyment of foundation paper piecing.

HOW TO PAPER PIECE

This section describes my method for foundation paper piecing, so refer to it when making the projects. All patterns referred to can be found in the PDF download.

Printing Patterns

It is important to check your printer settings every time that you print a foundation paper-pieced pattern, as failure to do so can result in your finished quilt having the wrong dimensions. The exact wording used in print preferences settings can vary greatly depending on your printer, the software you are using and many other factors. It is difficult to say exactly which settings you should use. You need to print using 'print 100%' or 'Actual Size'. Do *not* use 'Shrink to Size' or 'Fit to Page'. Where possible, open the PDF in Adobe Reader, as this gives clear, unambiguous printing options. The pattern pieces have been formatted for Letter size paper, but will print on A4 without issue, on condition that the correct printer settings are used. A 1in square has been printed on the first page of each individual pattern. Always measure this before you start sewing to check whether your pattern has accidentally been reduced in size.

Resizing Patterns

One of the fun things about paper-pieced patterns is that it is relatively easy to alter the dimensions of a pattern. That said, it is worth considering that not every pattern should be altered in size. There is often a very good reason that a designer has decided to make a pattern a specific size. By reducing the size of patterns, pieces can sometimes become ridiculously small and by increasing the size, pieces can become rather unwieldy to sew. As a result, it may be that patterns that have been reduced or enlarged in size must be altered slightly to accommodate this change.

The table below gives an overview of the percentages that you can use to alter the size of a block. For example, if you want to enlarge a 4in block to a 10in block, set the scale to 250% when printing or photocopying the pattern. If you want to decrease the size of an 8in block and turn it into a 6in block, set the scale to 75%. The basic equation for working out these numbers is:
what you want (required block size) ÷ what you have (current block size) x 100.

There is one final step to take when changing the size of a pattern. Increasing or decreasing a pattern will alter the size of the *whole* paper foundation, including the ¼in seam allowance. It is very important therefore to manually change the seam allowances back to ¼in. When decreasing the size of a pattern, it may be necessary to cut the page and separate the pattern pieces before decreasing the size on a photocopier. In this way, you can leave enough room on the page to allow for enlarged seam allowances.

							Required Block Size (in inches)												
	4	**6**	**8**	**10**	**12**	**14**	**16**	**18**	**20**	**22**	**24**	**26**	**28**	**30**	**32**	**34**	**36**	**38**	**40**
4	100	150	200	250	300	350	400	450	500	550	600	650	700	750	800	850	900	950	1000
6	67	100	133	167	200	233	267	300	333	367	400	433	467	500	533	567	600	633	667
8	50	75	100	125	150	175	200	225	250	275	300	325	350	375	400	425	450	475	500
10	40	60	80	100	120	140	160	180	200	220	240	260	280	300	320	340	360	380	400
12	33	50	67	84	100	117	133	150	167	184	200	217	233	250	267	284	300	317	333
14	29	43	57	71	86	100	114	129	143	157	171	186	200	214	229	243	257	271	286
16	25	38	50	63	75	88	100	113	125	138	150	163	175	188	200	213	225	238	250
18	22	33	44	56	67	78	89	100	111	122	133	144	156	167	178	189	200	211	222
20	20	30	40	50	60	70	80	90	100	110	120	130	140	150	160	170	180	190	200
22	18	27	36	45	55	64	73	82	91	100	109	118	127	136	145	155	164	173	182
24	17	25	33	42	50	58	67	75	83	92	100	108	117	125	133	142	150	158	167
26	15	23	31	38	46	54	62	69	77	85	92	100	108	115	123	131	138	146	154
28	14	21	29	36	43	50	57	64	71	79	86	93	100	107	114	121	129	136	143
30	13	20	26	33	40	47	53	60	67	73	80	87	93	100	107	113	120	126	133
32	13	19	25	31	38	44	50	56	63	69	75	82	88	94	100	106	113	119	125
34	12	18	24	29	35	41	47	53	59	65	71	76	82	88	94	100	106	112	118
36	11	17	22	28	33	39	44	50	56	61	67	72	78	83	89	94	100	106	111
38	11	16	21	26	32	37	42	47	53	58	63	68	73	79	84	89	95	100	105
40	10	15	20	25	30	35	40	45	50	55	60	65	70	75	80	85	90	95	100

(Row labels under **Current Block Size**)

Assembling Paper Templates

Each paper template has a ¼in seam allowance around the edge and when you cut the template out, this is the line that you will cut along. Some paper templates are small enough to be printed on a single sheet of paper (see **Photo 1**). Some templates are so large that they span a few pages and will need to be glued together. It is important that you check the pattern instructions *before* gluing the templates, as sometimes it is best to wait until after the first few fabric pieces have been sewn before you completely glue them together. By waiting to construct your paper foundation, you make it easier to reach and sew small fabric pieces in the centre of the paper template. When gluing pieces together, lay the red dashed lines on top of each other. If you have positioned the pieces correctly, you will see that the lines of the pattern line up beautifully, as shown by the blue lines in **Photos 2** and **3**. I tend to use a stationery-grade glue stick to glue my papers together. Beware of using adhesive tape as it can melt when heated by an iron, leading to a nasty mess on your ironing board.

Stitch Length

When you are ready to start paper piecing, you will need to reduce the length of your stitches. Stitch sizes can vary depending on the sewing machine, but for most machines aim for a stitch length between 1.5 and 2. The stitches should be close together, but not so close that they shred the paper. The small stitch length creates a line of small perforations along the paper, meaning that there is minimal strain placed on the stitches when the paper is torn away.

Working in Reverse

When discussing paper piecing, I often hear people comment that they find it confusing and 'back-to-front'. The reason for this is that the paper templates show the pattern in reverse. The printed.paper template is behind the sewing and faces backwards, thus it is in mirror image to the sewing that is being produced. While this can be a source of confusion to some, it is worth remembering that the actual process of sewing is no different to other kinds of patchwork. Place two pieces of fabric with right sides together and sew the seam. The only thing that is extra is a piece of paper and a printed line to give you guidance.

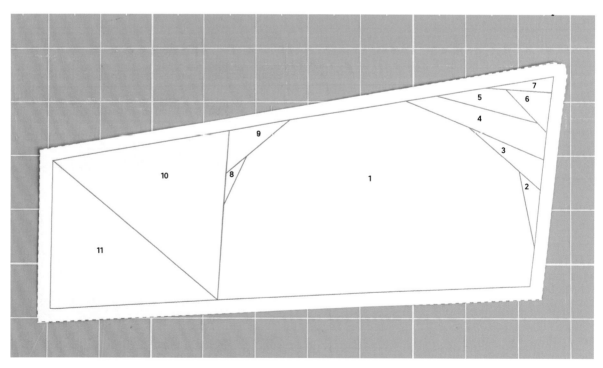

PHOTO 1

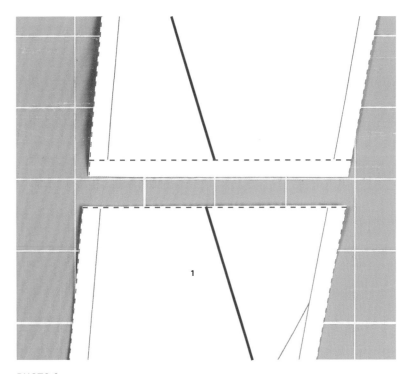

PHOTO 2

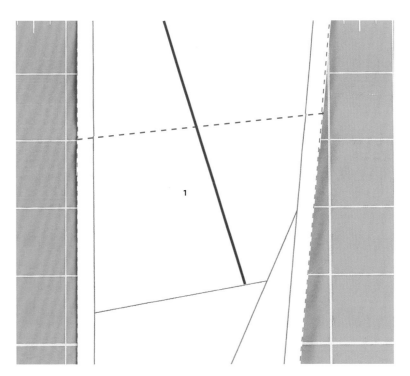

PHOTO 3

PAPER PIECING PROCESS

Refer to this section when foundation piecing the projects to remind you of the basic process. Red thread has been used in the photos shown in this section, so the stitches can be seen clearly.

1 Getting Started

Each paper piece is numbered. Start piecing from number one and work through all the numbers systematically until you are finished. When I teach paper piecing, I often find that the hardest aspect of piecing for people to get to grips with is the very first piece. The logic of it is just a little bit different and can seem confusing. Once past the first piece, the process is repetitive and it is a question of finding your groove. Whenever you cut fabric for paper piecing, make sure that it is approximately ½in larger than the printed shape on the paper foundation. You do not need to cut precisely. I tend to always cut rectangles of fabric and then I reuse the scraps later in my project to minimize wastage. Some people like to cut all their fabric before they piece. I like to keep making creative decisions all the way through my project, so I cut as I sew.

2 Cut Fabric for Piece Number 1

Place the paper foundation printed side down on the table or light box. Place the fabric for piece 1 *right side up* on top of the paper foundation. If you are not using a light box, hold the paper and fabric up to the light with the paper template towards you, so that you can clearly see the printed lines and the outlines of the fabric pieces. Ensure that the fabric overlaps the edges of piece 1 by *at least ¼*in in all directions (**Photo 4**). If piece 1 is next to the printed seam allowance around the paper foundation, the fabric should also cover the seam allowance. When you are satisfied with the positioning of your fabric, place a pin to hold it in place. Try to ensure that the pin is far enough away from the line between piece 1 and 2, so it can stay in place while you are sewing the first seam.

3 Align

Place the fabric for piece 2 *right side down* on top of fabric piece number 1 (**Photo 5**). Carefully lift the whole pile up to the light again (or use the light box) to check that the majority of the fabric is on top of piece 1, but that the edge overlaps the printed line between piece 1 and 2 by more than ¼in. Check the position in one of the following ways.

- Gently fold the fabric of piece 2 back with your fingers. This can be a bit tricky to do if you are not used to it.

- Place a pin along the line that you are going to sew and then fold the fabric of piece 2 back.

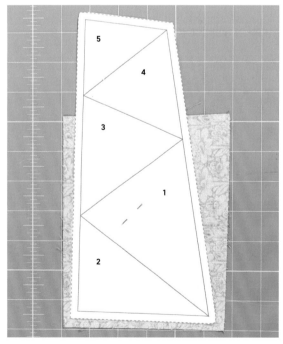

PHOTO 4

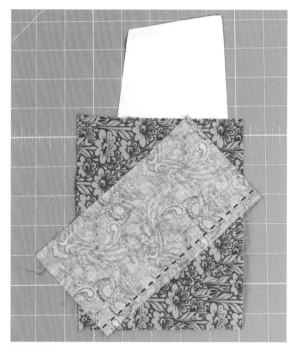

PHOTO 5

- Increase your stitch length to size 4 or larger and tack (baste) the seam. If you are happy with the positioning of the fabrics, you can resew the seam with your usual small paper piecing stitches. If you are not happy, then you can easily unpick the stitches and resew without worrying that you have weakened your paper foundation. This technique is especially useful when you are working with large-scale patterns or are trying to fussy cut fabrics. If you use this technique, try to develop a little internal alarm system – if you go to sew the next seam and your machine is still set to the large stitch length, go back and check that you have resewn the seam with small stitches.

4 Sew

Carefully manoeuvre your pile of fabric and paper into your sewing machine. Ensure that it is printed paper side *up* and that none of the fabrics move as you position it in the machine. If there is a corner of fabric that is in danger of flopping out of position and folding itself into the line of sewing, do not be scared to pin it to the paper template. You are going to sew down the line between piece 1 and piece 2 (**Photo 6**). It is important that you anchor your stitches so that they do not come undone when you remove the paper. There are a couple of ways to do this.

- Start and end your seams with a few backwards stitches. The disadvantage of this technique is that it makes the first few stitches harder to unpick.

- Start and finish your seam up to a ¼in past the end of the line. When you do this, you will need to rip the paper slightly when you fold it to trim the fabrics afterwards. This may not be suitable for areas of small piecing, such as in the eye areas of birds.

- A combination of the two. I often start my seams just before the start of the line and use a few backwards stitches.

If the line that is being sewn starts or finishes by the ¼in seam allowance, extend the line of stitches into the seam allowance. After you have sewn your seam, trim the tail of the thread to the paper.

5 Flip and Check

Gently fold the fabric for piece 2 over (**Photo 7**). Hold it up to the light and ensure that it generously covers paper shape 2, allowing at least ¼in seam allowances. If it doesn't, *carefully* unpick. If it does, then unfold fabric piece 2, let it lie on top of piece 1 again. Do *not* press yet.

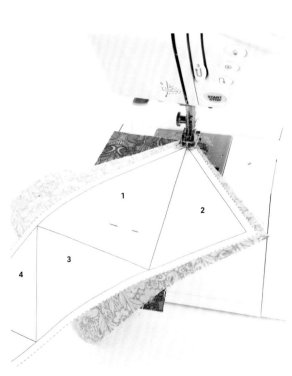

PHOTO 6

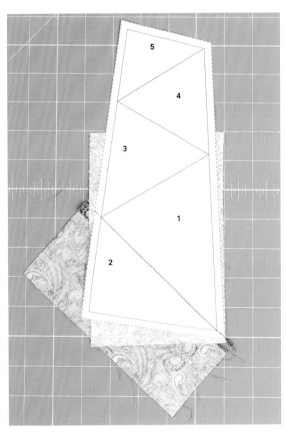

PHOTO 7

6 Trim

Ensuring that the two pieces of fabric that have just been sewn are lying facing each other, fold the paper back along the stitched lines so that the seam allowances are exposed. Place the ruler along the seam and trim the edges, allowing a ¼in seam allowance. **Photo 8** shows an Add-A-Quarter ruler being used, but a normal quilting ruler can be used.

7 Press

Lay your paper flat again. When pressing the seams, use a dry iron. There are two reasons for this – steam can distort the fabric and paper, and can lead to printed paper losing its ink and smudging black marks all over your beautiful sewing. It is a good idea to set the seam when pressing (**Photo 9**). This is done by pressing the seam flat, on the back of the fabric in the position that you have just sewn it. The next step is to open the seam and press again from the front (**Photo 10**). You can gently finger press the seam open before you press, to ensure that the crease lands in the correct spot.

8 Repeat

Repeat the basic process from Step 3 Align, until you have sewn all the fabric pieces to the paper foundation. Repeat this process on all of the paper foundations of the design. Once all the fabrics have been sewn to the paper template, trim the fabrics to the seam allowance (the outer line on each template). If it is essential that the finished block is exactly the right size, I recommend *not* trimming the outer edge of the block until all the sections have been sewn together. If you are in danger of forgetting this while you sew, then place a brightly coloured line in the paper seam allowance of the outer edge and this will serve as a memory aid.

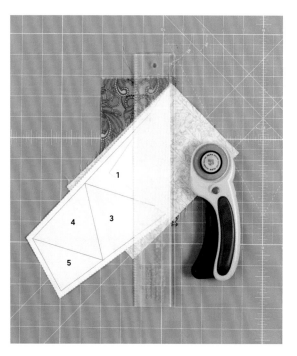

PHOTO 8

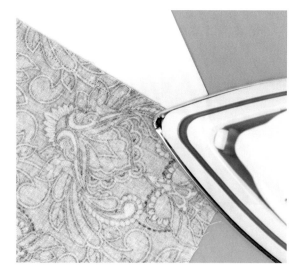

PHOTO 9

PHOTO 10

PERFECTING THE TECHNIQUE

We have now covered the basics of paper piecing, but there are definitely some aspects of the technique that take more practise than others. These are the things that make the difference between you enjoying paper piecing and wanting to throw your sewing across the room!

Sewing Awkward Angles

To achieve the level of detail that I want in my work, my patterns tend to have some pieces with awkward angles. Here is my advice on dealing with these.

1 Cut a piece of fabric that is at least ½in larger in all directions than the area you want to cover. Lay your paper template printed side up on your ironing board. Lay the fabric rectangle right side down on the printed side of the template. Ensure that it generously covers the section that you want to sew and that you have left enough fabric for seam allowances. Fold the fabric along the seam that you are going to sew and press (**Photo 11**). Take note of the position of the fabric in relation to the template (the dashed line on **Photo 11** indicates the template edges). It is important to know how much fabric overhang there is at either end, as this will help you position the fabric correctly against the non-printed side of the template. You may choose to mark the ends of the section on the fabric with a fabric marker.

2 Now take the fabric and position it in situ against the non-printed side of the paper template (**Photo 12**). Remember that it will be placed right sides together with the fabric of the area adjacent to the area you are about to cover. Hold the paper foundation and the new fabric piece up to the light and check that the fold of the fabric follows the line that you are about to sew. When happy with the positioning, flick the fold of the fabric open (**Photo 13**) and then position the whole bundle in your sewing machine ready to sew (**Photo 14**). In cases where you are piecing an area next to the edge of the paper and the fabric that you are about to sew is visible around the edges of the paper template, it is possible to make a final check on fabric alignment. Look for the crease that was created when you pressed the fabric and check whether it is still in alignment with the printed line. If you look at **Photo 14** you will see that the fabric needs to be moved a couple of millimetres to the right (see arrow).

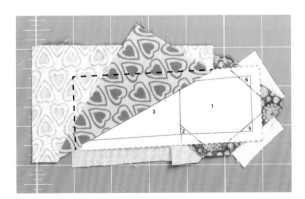

PHOTO 11

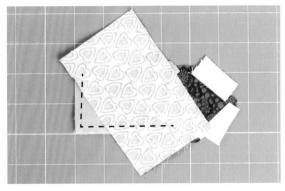

PHOTO 13

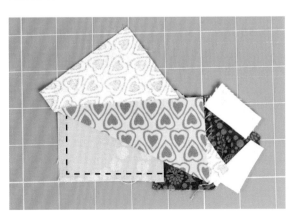

PHOTO 12

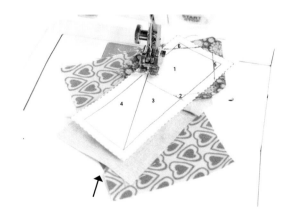

PHOTO 14

3 Sew along the line with a large tacking (basting) stitch (**Photo 15**). Check whether the fabric piece has been orientated correctly. If not, unpick the stitches and try again. If it has been sewn correctly, resew the line using your normal small paper piecing stitches.

Sewing with Directional Prints

When sewing with directional prints (such as text prints), I tend to stop and think before I start sewing. Do I want the background to be fractured and haphazard with the print going in all directions? Or is it important to line the designs up neatly in a horizontal direction? I often take the haphazard approach, but there are definitely times, such as the Monarch Butterfly quilt, when it is worth making the extra effort to align a directional print accurately.

1 Lay the paper foundations out in their correct positions. Draw an arrow pointing straight up towards the upper edge of the paper. This arrow will act as a constant reminder as to where the top of the block lies. Now draw a horizontal line that can be used as a reference for accurate alignment (**Photo 16**).

2 Cut fabric generously, bearing its orientation in mind.

3 Lay the paper template print side up on the ironing board. Lay the fabric right side down over the area that you wish to sew. Use the drawn reference line to help orientate the fabric accurately. Fold the seam allowance along the line that you will sew. Press to create a nice clean edge.

4 Move the fabric to the non-printed side of the template. Hold paper and fabric up to the light and align the fold with the printed line. Sew using tacking (basting) stitches.

5 Check that the alignment is accurate and resew the seam using small stitches.

Working with Large Paper Foundations

Large paper foundations can be difficult to deal with. It can be tricky to hold small pieces of fabric in position, reaching the small sections in the centre of the page can be tough and it can be virtually impossible to manoeuvre them all into the machine while keeping everything in position. It is important to *read the project instructions* before assembling your paper template. Often, it is easier to sew some of the fabric pieces before gluing the whole paper template together, as by so doing, many of the pieces become more accessible and easier to sew. I try not to fold my paper foundation, as folds and creases make it harder to manage. Pins are your friends, so don't be afraid to pin fabric in position.

Working with Large Fabric Pieces

Large pieces of fabric can be tricky when paper piecing. They can warp, drag, pull away from the paper and generally be difficult to manage.

1 Make sure that you have a work surface that is big enough for you to lay the whole paper foundation flat and that there is enough space around your machine so your sewing is not obstructed. By so doing, it will become easier to judge the size of the fabric required and will help you to position it accurately.

2 Press all fabric pieces before sewing them. This is something that I do for all paper piecing, but it is especially important when dealing with large fabric pieces.

PHOTO 15

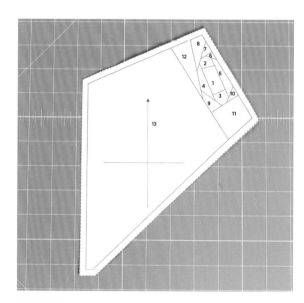

PHOTO 16

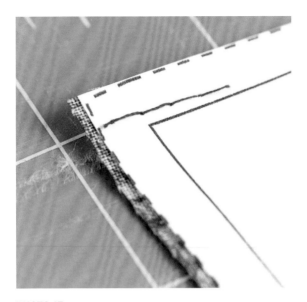

PHOTO 17

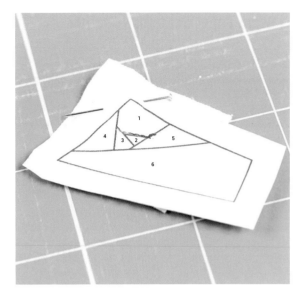

PHOTO 18

3 I strongly recommend that you use pins and or glue to help attach the fabric to the paper foundations. Another tip that can really help is to place a few large tacking (basting) stitches in the seam allowances (**Photo 17**). This will help to ensure that the fabric stays in the correct place.

4 When cutting your fabric, be more generous than you would be for small pieces. I admit that this will lead to the formation of extra fabric scraps, but you can reuse these in other areas of your block. If I am worried that I may run out of fabric, I will often start with the largest foundations, so that I can cut my fabric generously and then use the off-cuts in later, smaller sections of the pattern.

Working with Small Fabric Pieces

Areas of intense piecing with many small fabric pieces can easily become very bulky due to the build-up of layers of seam allowances. If this becomes a problem, it is possible to trim the seam allowances slightly narrower making them between ⅛in and ¼in. This is not something that I do regularly, as I am slightly nervous about seams popping, but there are times when it is necessary, especially when I am confident that the fabric will be held in place by multiple seams. When the first two pieces

of fabric to be sewn to a paper template are small, the stitches can sometimes rip away from the paper, leading to frustration and resewing. In such cases follow these simple steps.

1 It is important to be gentle. I would recommend that you do not pre-cut your fabric too accurately. By so doing, there will be minimal additional fabric wastage but you give yourself breathing space.

2 Be sure to use a pin to anchor fabric piece 1 to the paper and if possible try to ensure that this pin can remain in situ until the seam between piece 2 and 3 has been sewn (**Photo 18**). As there will only be a small number of stitches holding the fabric to the paper, this pin serves to take some of the strain off the seam between piece 1 and piece 2 and means that there is less chance that the stitches will rip away from the paper.

3 Start the seam one or two stitches before the line begins and extend it one or two stitches past the end. These few extra stitches can make all the difference in anchoring the fabric to the paper.

4 Take care when folding the fabric, as there are only a few anchor stitches and it's easy to misalign the fold.

Sewing Paper Sections Together

Every paper-pieced pattern in this book consists of multiple paper foundations (lettered A, B, C, etc) and these must be sewn together in the correct order to create a finished quilt top. The order that the foundations are joined is important and every pattern has a list that gives the sequence in which they should be sewn together. The difference between a mediocre and an expert piece of paper piecing often lies in the accuracy with which the individual paper pieces are sewn together, so it is definitely worth taking the time to do this as accurately as possible. I think that much of the groundwork for perfectly aligned seams is done while you are piecing each section. I know that opinions in the paper piecing world are split as to whether it is necessary to press every seam with an iron as you sew, but I have found that pressing seams adds accuracy to my piecing. I have tried to be lazy and to finger press my seams, but each time I have found that the fabrics have not creased in quite the right place and that this has led to inaccuracy when it comes to matching seams. It may be that this is the fault of my finger pressing technique (or lack of it) but experience has taught me that it is best to be cautious and to press every seam.

I like to use a walking foot when I sew paper templates together. I have found that the papers are less likely to slip in relation to each other and alignment is just that bit more accurate when sewn this way.

1 The first thing that you should do is to analyze the pattern. You will notice that there are some sections that can easily be sewn together without any need for precision, while others require significantly more attention to detail. When I consider each pattern, I look for the critical joining points – these are the points that need to match precisely when they are sewn together. Examples of these joining points are shown by red circles in **Fig 1**.

2 Once you have identified a critical joining point, push a pin through the paper and straight through to the fabric (**Photo 19**). Make sure that the pin comes out directly adjacent to the crease of the seam (**Photo 20**). Now take the other paper template and continue to push the pin through the crease of the fabric and the paper of the template (**Photo 21**). When you have done this, the pin should be standing perpendicular to the papers, which are sandwiched together with fabric in the centre (**Photo 22**). I call this pin the anchor pin. If you now take the anchor pin and push it through the paper horizontally, you will notice that the papers shift on top of each other and are no longer beautifully lined up (**Photo 23**). Even the slightest movement of the papers at this stage can make a huge difference to the accuracy of your join. As a result, you need to leave the anchor pin standing perpendicular to the fabric for the moment.

FIG 1

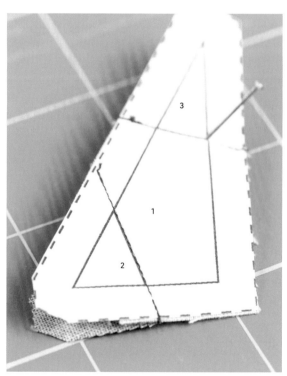

PHOTO 19

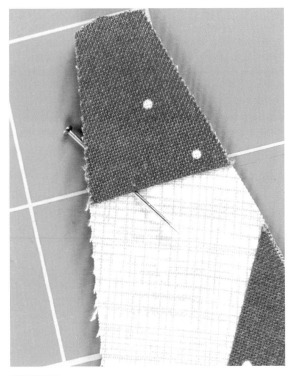

PHOTO 20

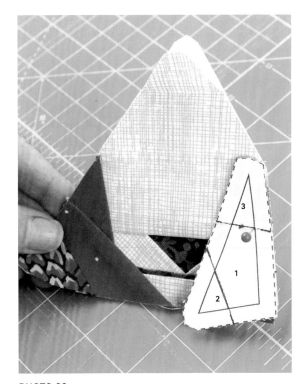

PHOTO 22

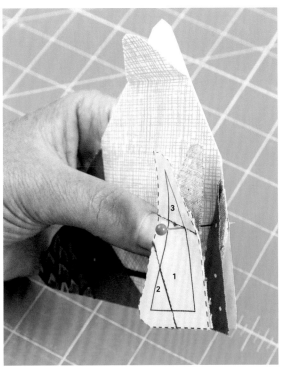

PHOTO 21

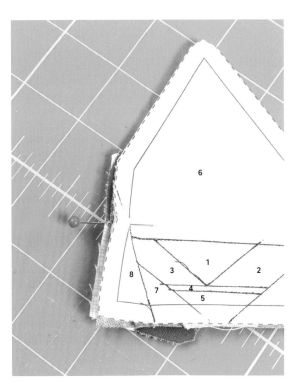

PHOTO 23

3 Use Clover Wonder Clips or pins to anchor the papers together on either side of the anchor pin. If you so choose, you can take the anchor pin out (or if you are cautious like me, you can leave it in, but please don't blame me if you end up with a scratched sewing machine!). If there are several critical anchor points along one seam, place anchor pins on every one of these points. Anchor pins can also be helpful at the start and finish of seams, especially when sewing a paper with an acute angle.

4 When sewing your papers together there is nothing more annoying than making a mistake and having to unpick thousands of tiny stitches. For this reason, I strongly recommend that you increase your stitch length to 4 or even larger and tack (baste) the seam before sewing it properly. Not only does tacking (basting) make it easier to remove inaccurate stitches, but it also protects your paper. Shredding the paper by stitching it multiple times only makes it harder to sew the seam accurately. Start sewing from the end closest to the first anchor pin. The shorter the distance that you have to sew before crossing an anchor point, the smaller the chance that slippage will occur and the more accurately you will sew. An easy way to judge the accuracy of your tacked (basted) seam is to look at the stitches in relation to the printed pattern. Do the stitches follow the lines or do they veer off into space? Remember that it is not just a question of aligning papers, you also need to ensure that the fabric is also lined up with your papers and that a ¼in seam of fabric has been sewn as well as a ¼in of paper. Sometimes shifting the alignment of your paper by a mere millimetre can make a huge difference to the alignment of critical join points, especially when joining a point where one of the seams hits the join point at an acute angle. At other times, the first part of a seam will be beautifully aligned, but the second part goes awry. In this case, I will often only unpick the tacking (basting) stitches from the second part of the seam and will then resew that part of the seam. If you have sewn a seam several times and it is still not lining up correctly, it may be an idea to carry the papers to the machine with the anchor pin still in situ. Carefully drop your sewing machine needle into the exact position that your anchor pin stands (removing the pin as you do this). Tack (baste) from this point to the end of your seam, and then return to the original position of the anchor pin and sew in the other direction.

5 In general, I press the seams between sections closed. The sections will almost always decide for themselves which way that they want to lie. That said, at times (especially when the critical join point falls on a steeply angled seam where there is a lot of bulk), you may find that a seam has been joined accurately, but doesn't look right. In this case the bulk of seam allowance, which has been pressed closed, may affect the lie of the fabric and make the join look inaccurate. It is worth checking to see whether opening the seam will make a difference. Sharing the bulk between the two sides of the seam is a subtle change but can make all the difference.

6 Once you are happy with your tacked (basted) seam, don't forget to immediately go back and sew it again with your small paper piecing stitches. Try to train a little alarm bell in your head to warn that if you start sewing the next seam and your machine sews with a tacking (basting) stitch, something is wrong. Go back and check if you remembered to sew over your tacking (basting) stitches on the last seam. Another good habit to get into is to rip about an inch of paper away from the ends of the seam allowances once you have sewn two sections together (**Photo 24**). By so doing, you decrease the bulk of the seam allowances and make it significantly easier to remove the papers from your finished block. If you prefer, you can remove the paper from the length of the seam allowance, but personally I love the extra security that is given by leaving part of the seam allowance paper in situ.

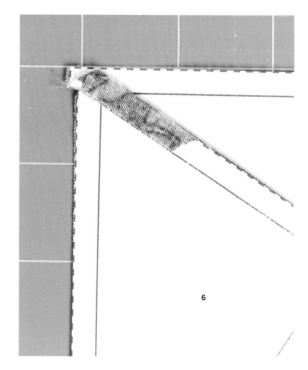

PHOTO 24

Removing Papers

Only remove the papers once you have finished a complete block and are ready to either tack (baste) the quilt or sew on borders. Remember that a paper-pieced block can be vulnerable to warping as the fabrics are generally sewn in all directions, so be very gentle with your finished top. In general, there are no great tricks as to how to remove papers. Take your time, do it gently and rip the pieces in reverse number order. At times, it can be helpful to have a pair of tweezers or a quick unpick to help ease some of the smaller paper pieces out of the seams.

Finishing a Block

When a block is finished, it can appear a bit lumpy along the seams. Points where multiple seams join up can lead to unsightly lumps and bumps. The discrepancy in the thickness of the seams can make it difficult to gain a neat result when pressing the finished block. The thick areas can become shiny, the thin areas sag and the whole block just looks tortured. A final step can help to flatten your seams out and give your block a more professional and finished look. Once all the papers are removed, have a quick look at the back of your block. Ensure that all the seams are pressed in the directions that you want them to be, if not, place the block seams side up and press them quickly into position. Lay several layers of wadding (batting) on your ironing board. Place your block on top of the wadding (batting) with the right side facing up, seam side down. Spray the block generously with starch or starch equivalent and then press the block until it is dry. By doing this you will see that the block becomes beautifully flat, with crisp seams and all seams pressed down into the wadding (batting). Using starch has the added bonus of protecting the block from warping.

FABRIC SELECTION

Fabric selection can be crucial when sewing a pictorial paper-pieced pattern. In this chapter I will shy away from creating hard and fast fabric selection rules as I don't think they are helpful. I used to create rules for myself, but I gave up on them when I realized that I was forever breaking them! As I continue on my quilting journey, I am continually improving my skills and discovering more adventurous ways to use fabric prints. So, instead of creating a set of useless rules, I will talk you through some of the aspects of fabric selection that can be considered when choosing fabrics and will also discuss the potential pitfalls of bad choices.

PATTERN GUIDANCE

My passion for quilt design stems from the fact that I love seeing the beautiful creations that people produce with my patterns. It constantly blows my mind to see the imaginative ways in which people interpret the designs with their fabric selection. I find it fascinating how people see different things in the patterns and choose to highlight contrasting aspects of the designs.

When I sit down and translate a design to a paper pattern, I try to respect the different ways people might interpret the designs. I don't want the patterns to be written in a restrictive way that will limit the creativity of others, but at the same time I don't want to leave people floundering and completely without guidance. I see myself walking a fine line between dictating how I want you to interpret a pattern, giving sufficient guidance to those who require it and allowing others the freedom to do as they wish. I hope that you feel that I cut the right line. **Fig 1** shows an example of three different interpretations of colour choices in a design. All three versions work perfectly and, depending on the available fabric, each could be used to create a stunning quit.

I choose not to colour or shade the pattern pieces of my designs, and there are several reasons for this.

- Shading makes it harder to see through the paper when piecing, which can make the process more difficult, especially when working with dark fabrics.

- There are only a limited number of shades of grey available in my design software. Often there are too few to accurately represent all the colours that are required.

- Shading can become confusing if you choose not to follow it. Imagine if I had coloured the pattern of a black sheep, but you wanted to sew a white sheep. I tried this once and let's just say that there was a lot of unpicking done that day!

- Finally, and perhaps most importantly, I am very aware that there are many different ways to interpret my patterns. It doesn't feel right for me to limit your interpretations. Shading the pattern pieces leaves less room for your own creativity.

FIG 1

I feel that it is my job to provide guidance and to help you to create the best possible results. When doing my own sewing, where necessary, I use letters and/or words to mark the pattern with suggested fabric placement information, and you could do the same. Use the various diagrams as reference. A little bit of preparation before you start sewing can save a lot of heartache later in the process. In the Panda pattern for example, you could mark the black and white pieces, and the background too if you wish. In some projects, I have made suggestions in the text as to possible pitfalls of the fractured background.

QUILT PLANNING

I have to admit that when it comes to starting new projects, my natural tendency is to impetuously jump in with both feet. This a fun and exciting way to work, but it has led to more than a few disastrous fabric choices. Over the years, I have had to teach myself to stop and consider my fabric selections and I have learnt to love mulling over fabric options. I have come to recognize that making considered fabric choices is an important part of the quilting process and one that I really enjoy. I would suggest that it is especially crucial when sewing large-scale paper-pieced patterns.

If this is all a bit new to you, then my first piece of advice is very important – don't be intimidated! We all make mistakes. There is nothing wrong with making mistakes, as long as we learn from them. Look at the quilts that you have already sewn in your quilting journey. Are

there fabric selections that you regret? Can you put your finger on why these choices don't work? Try to analyze your mistakes, but embrace them at the same time. The whole point of this exercise is not to make you regret your previous choices, but to try and improve your skills. Don't just analyze what didn't work, think about what *did* work. What do you love about specific quilts? Why do their fabrics work so well?

There are a number of different ways to plan your fabric choices, and each has its own pros and cons. I suggest that you try a variety of these methods and find the one or ones that work for you. Many people find that shading the Colouring Charts provided with each project is time well spent. These sheets provide a means of playing with the composition of a block. Maybe you want to test if a dark background would work, or you have a completely radical colour palette in your head. The Colouring Chart offers the possibility to try out these different interpretations of the pattern (**Photo 1**). While colouring, it is important to be mindful of the fabrics that you have. Don't colour the background purple unless you have a similarly coloured fabric in mind.

I think that one of the best uses for the Colouring Chart is to see if different fabric placement strategies work. Remember, you don't have to religiously follow every fabric placement suggestion that I make. Sometimes you may want to add more subtle shading or to limit the colour palette. Don't be afraid to play around with these ideas – add more subtlety or remove it as it suits. I can often think of numerous different interpretations of a pattern, but can only show a small number of these in the book.

PHOTO 1

PHOTO 2

If you prefer, you could cut slivers of your fabrics and stick them to the chart (see **Photo 2**). This is not a technique that I personally use, as I worry that by cutting a sliver, only a small area of the fabric is represented and, depending on the scale of the fabric design, this can lead to bad fabric choices. It is a technique that is best suited to small-scale prints and solids, as it can mask distracting elements in larger-scale prints.

My favourite method is to start by cutting out the paper templates and laying the fabrics out in piles on top of them, so I can see how they all work together (**Photo 3**). I fold and overlap the fabrics, mimicking the layout of the quilt and placing the correct fabrics adjacent to each other. Once the fabrics have been laid out, I look at them close up and from a distance. I take photographs. I go away, make a cup of tea, return and have another look. If something is jarring or if I have doubts about a specific fabric, then I will swap in another fabric and try again. It really is important to keep playing until I am happy. Once I have made my decisions, I write notes on the paper templates to remind me of my chosen fabrics.

COLOUR VALUE

Some fabrics seem like a good idea when you are initially choosing them, but when you lay them next to other fabrics they lose all of their impact. This often occurs because the colour value is too similar. Colour value refers to the lightness or darkness of a colour, indicating the quantity of light reflected. It is not always immediately obvious to the naked eye, but there are a couple of tricks that you can use to make sure that the fabrics you choose have distinct colour values. There is nothing more frustrating than piecing a detail, only to discover that it disappears into the background fabric. In general, my philosophy is that I don't want to go to the trouble of piecing a quilt if the details will disappear and can't be seen.

PHOTO 3

Once you think that you have chosen your fabrics, lay them out and take a photo on your phone (**Photo 4**). It helps if you ensure that fabrics that will be adjacent to each other in the final layout are positioned next to each other. Seeing the fabrics laid together in miniature can sometimes give a different perspective and can show whether the fabrics really work together.

If you remain unsure as to whether the fabrics work together, put a black and white filter over your photo and look carefully (**Photo 5**). A simple way to apply a filter is using Instagram, but there are a whole variety of other photo editing apps that easily do the job. Once the filter has been applied, the most surprising fabrics can sometimes become indistinguishable and others can stand out far more than anticipated. The colour value test is a technique that I have really grown to trust. I have overruled it a few times and each time I have regretted it. A further advantage of photographing your progress is that it documents the process, which means that you can refer back to the photos as and when necessary.

I tested the colour value of fabrics many, many times while sewing the quilts for this book. Each quilt represents a significant investment of time and fabric, so it was important to me that my fabric decisions were as good as possible. When piecing the Panda quilt for example, I divided the fabrics into three groups – white, black and mid-tone. Using low-volume prints too close to the panda would have blurred its outline and made it less easily recognizable. The same could be said if I placed navy and other high-value fabrics close to the panda. I wanted the panda to be immediately recognizable and the best way to do this was by surrounding it with mid-value fabrics.

When sewing the Howl quilt, I had two fat eighth bundles of Oakshott cottons. I laid all of the fabrics on the black background fabric and took a photo. This showed me that while it was fine to use all of the red tones, three of the blue tones were too dark and would detract from the details of my quilt. I am so glad that I did this test before I started sewing. I would have been very disappointed if I had sewn the whole quilt, only to see that the outline was obscured by bad fabric choices.

PHOTO 4

PHOTO 5

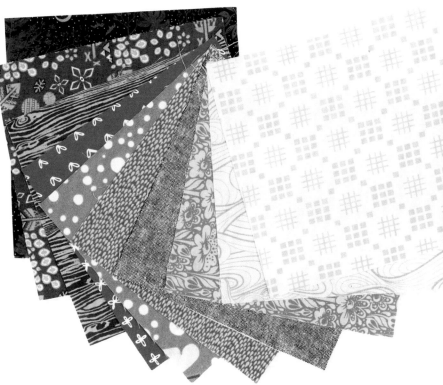

DISTRACTING PRINTS

While busy prints can be fun, I am often cautious of them. As I have already said, I don't want the piecing that I do to be overshadowed by bad fabric choices. Loud, busy prints can be disastrous when applied without care. While it is definitely true that large polka dots and novelty prints can be fun to sew and have more than earned their place in quilting, I would argue that they should be used sparingly and deliberately in the kind of pictorial paper piecing that I do. Busy fabrics can interfere with the overall appearance of your quilt and can all too easily overshadow the pieced detail. In general, the fabrics that I am drawn to are those that read as one dominant colour, rather than a riot of contrasting colours.

If you choose to use busy prints, try to balance them with other calmer fabrics, so the eye has somewhere to rest. Be very conscious of where you place them and consider whether they will distract from the overall picture that you are trying to create. I must admit that one of the fabrics that I used had a beautiful blue background and green details. It was absolutely perfect for my Peacock quilt, except for the large purple flowers that were dotted across the fabric. Although beautiful, these flowers were unsuitable for my purpose and would have distracted from the image that I was trying to create. When cutting the fabric pieces for my quilt, I deliberately cut around this distracting element. There are no purple flowers in my quilt, but I was able to utilize the texture of the background print in the fabric perfectly and I'm very pleased with the result.

It is worth being cautious when using a background fabric that has design detail in the same colour as the subject of the quilt. If that detail falls along the junction between the animal and the background, it can smudge the outline and make the silhouette unclear (**Photo 6**). In order to combat this problem, in the finished Polar Bear quilt, the background fabrics that have white detail have all been kept away from the outline of the bear and have intentionally been kept to the outside of the quilt. As such, they do not distract from the outline of the bear.

PHOTO 6

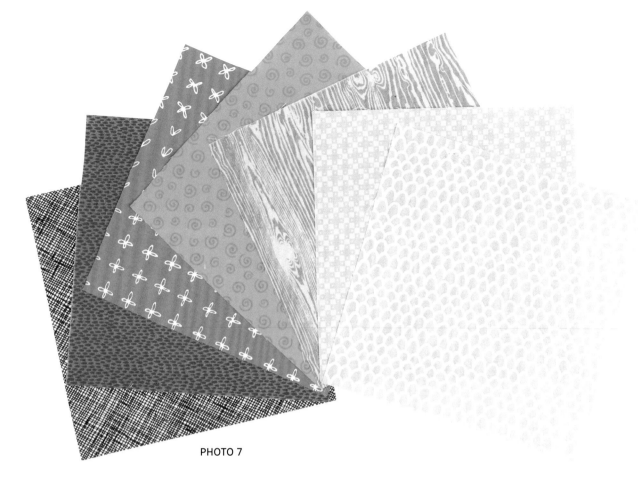

PHOTO 7

ADDING TEXTURE

I like to use fabrics that reflect the textures of the creature that I am sewing. I rarely use fabrics with large-scale geometric shapes in my animal quilts as straight lines seldom occur in nature. I tend to keep to more organic shapes with curves. Woodgrain, sketch, blender and tone-on-tone fabrics are some of my favourite fabrics to use (**Photo 7**).

Large-scale floral fabrics were used in the Peacock quilt. That said, to me they do not immediately read as flowers. They serve to give the bird texture and could almost be seen as feathers. I used low-volume fabrics for the swan, but was very selective in the prints used. Where possible, I avoided prints with heavy black detail or colours that would be out of place, such as red, green and blue. Instead, I chose to use grey, tan, gold, silver and other similar tones. I did not want the swan to be completely flat through using solid fabrics, but it was important that the prints did not overpower the swan.

Don't forget to have fun with your fabric selections. The mouse-hunting barn owl (Hunted quilt) has a Lizzy House mouse represented among the feathers on the underside of his wing. If you search my quilts, you will often find fun details like this.

FABRIC SCALE

It is important to match the scale of your fabric to the scale of the pattern. As a rule of thumb, small-scale patterns work best with small-scale prints and solids. They can easily be overpowered by large-scale prints. When large-scale prints are used carelessly in small blocks, the fabric detail can be mistaken for pieced details. Try to keep your work clean and unambiguous. See **Photo 8** (overleaf) for examples of larger-scale fabric designs.

My love of large-scale paper piecing stems in part from the fact that larger pattern designs allow the use of a wider variety of fabrics. A whole world of fabrics that are not suitable for small-scale patterns suddenly become tempting. Prints that would overpower a 12in block can be the perfect scale for 30in and 40in designs. The bigger the pattern that you are sewing, the larger the scale of the fabric designs that you can safely use.

You will notice that the quilts in this book utilize a wide variety of scales of fabric design. In general, where large-scale prints have been used, they are fabrics that have a fairly uniform colour palette. The large scale of the print is calmed by the limited colour scheme that it represents. The fabric may have a large print, but it actually 'reads' as a single colour.

PHOTO 8

DIRECTIONAL PRINTS

Some fabrics, such as text prints, stripes and plaids have a definite orientation (**Photo 9**). Many paper piecers choose to avoid these fabrics at all costs or only use them for fussy-cut details. Others make the decision to ignore the directionality of the fabric and a final group embrace the directionality of the print and try to line the fabric up as carefully as possible. There is no right or wrong approach – your decision will depend on your personal taste and the effect that you are trying to create.

If you decide to embrace the directionality of the print and line it up as well as possible, there are a few factors that you must take into account. It is likely that you will need to increase the amount of fabric that you buy. Piecing a directional background in an intentional way means that there will be more fabric wastage than usual. Don't be scared to save your off-cuts, so you can use them in future projects.

When using a directional print in the background of a block, I strongly recommend that you invest some time in preparations – for advice refer back to Perfecting the Technique: Sewing with Directional Prints.

PHOTO 9

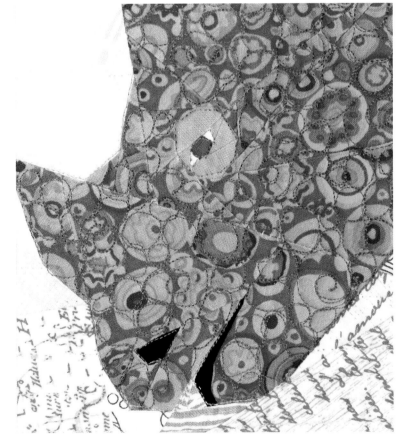

PROJECTS

PANDA

When I first started playing with the idea of compiling patterns for a book, I was tempted by the idea of creating a book with black and white animals depicted on colourful fractured backgrounds. I quickly decided that the brief was too restrictive and moved on to a wider concept, but this panda design stems from those early days.

FINISHED SIZES

Block: 20in x 20in

Quilt: 20in x 20in

FABRIC REQUIREMENTS

- ¼yd white fabric
- ⅜yd black fabric
- Variety of scraps for background (charm squares could be used)
- 24in x 24in wadding (batting)
- 24in x 24in backing fabric (¾yd)
- ⅛yd binding fabric

FABRIC CHOICES

This is the perfect pattern to sew if you want to reduce the scraps in your scrap bins.

When choosing the background fabrics, I strongly recommend that you consider colour values – see my advice in Fabric Selection: Colour Value. You need to have three different categories of colour – light shades for the white of the panda, dark shades for the black of the panda and mid shades for the background. To keep the panda silhouette crisp, try to keep the background fabrics to mid shades. Another thing to consider is that background prints with a lot of black or white can sometimes detract from the straight, sharp lines of paper piecing and can blur the clear outline you are creating – for advice see Fabric Selection: Distracting Prints.

Consider the effect that you want to create. If done carefully, a low-volume background could definitely work for this quilt. Quilting would play a big part in helping to distinguish the panda from the background. You could choose to create a gradient of colour or a random riot of colour, or to mask the borders of the fractured background by using busy prints and making the background appear like a jungle. When positioning background fabrics, try to look at the block as a whole. You do not have to use different fabrics for every single tiny piece – sometimes a better result can be gained by using the same fabric on two or three adjacent fabric pieces. Using the Colouring Chart will help you plan your block and make decisions.

PREPARATION

Find the relevant pages in the PDF. Print the patterns full size and check the 1in square is the correct size. Cut out the pattern pieces and use glue to assemble piece M. Take time to audition and select your fabrics and to study the diagrams.

Consider writing fabric placement notes on the pattern pieces. For example, you could write W for white, B for black and use words or letters to remind yourself which background fabric to position where. I often remind myself of the positioning of specific body parts by writing nose, ear, eye, etc. This serves as a reminder for those occasions when I decide to use a different shade to subtly distinguish specific features, such as the nose.

PIECING

Foundation piece the sections of the project (see Paper Piecing: Paper Piecing Process).

Once each section is pieced, sew them together in the following order:

A→B. C→D. AB→CD. ABCD→E. F→G. FG→H. FGH→I. ABCDE→FGHI. J→K. JK→L. ABCDEFGHI→JKL. ABCDEFGHIJKL→M. N→O. NO→P. NOP→Q. ABCDEFGHIJKLM→NOPQ. R→S. ABCDEFGHIJKLMNOPQ→RS.

When joining sections, note the critical join points and try to sew these points together as accurately as possible. See Perfecting the Technique: Sewing Paper Sections Together.

QUILT ASSEMBLY

Remove the papers. Press and starch the work (see Perfecting the Technique: Finishing a Block).

To make up as a mini quilt, prepare a quilt sandwich of the quilt, wadding (batting) and backing and quilt as desired (see General Techniques).

For the binding, cut two 2¼in x width of fabric strips and bind to finish (see General Techniques: Binding).

COLOURING CHART (REVERSE VIEW)

Potential Uses for this Block

CUSHION: When using a pictorial block to create a cushion, I generally like to add a small border. By so doing, the image is kept away from the edges of the cushion and no matter how fat the cushion filler, all details of the animal can be appreciated without the details around the edge being lost due to the curvature of the cushion. Border strips cut at 2in would work well for this pattern and would create a cushion to fit a 24in cushion insert. See General Techniques: Making a Cushion Cover.

CENTRAL BLOCK IN A MEDALLION QUILT: I would love to see this block used as the centre for a modern medallion quilt. I think it would be fresh, fun and colourful. The block itself suggests lots of fun colour combinations which could be utilized in the quilt.

MONARCH BUTTERFLY

The very first pattern I sold was a butterfly. It wasn't perfect, but it was very popular and for many years it was my best-selling pattern. It feels appropriate to revisit the butterfly, but this time to create a pattern that reflects my current design style. My children are fascinated by monarch butterflies and love watching them flit around the garden. For the first time, we have the correct vegetation in our garden and have the pleasure of watching the fascinating process of a simple egg becoming a caterpillar, then a chrysalis and finally a fragile butterfly. I guess it's no surprise that a monarch butterfly pattern is the result.

FINISHED SIZES

Block: 33in x 30in

Quilt: 40in x 50in

FABRIC REQUIREMENTS

- 1yd background fabric
- 1yd black fabric
- ⅝yd colour fabric for wings
- ⅛yd white fabric
- 1yd background fabric for borders
- 48in x 58in wadding (batting)
- 48in x 58in backing fabric (2¾yds)
- ⅜yd binding fabric

COLOUR DIAGRAM (REVERSE VIEW)

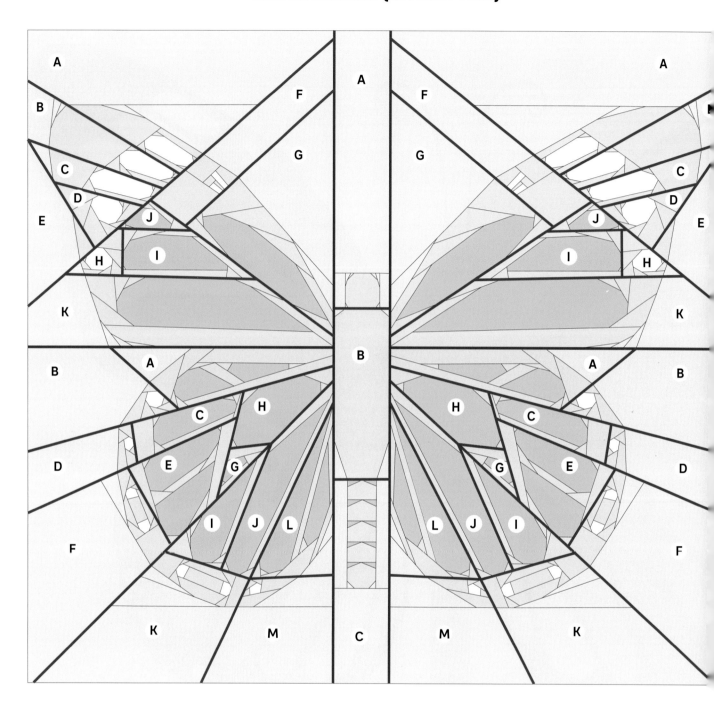

FABRIC CHOICES

If you are using a directional print in the background, more fabric may be necessary. If, like me, you are using ombre fabric, you may also require more fabric. I used ¼yd of a light to mid pink ombre and ½yd mid to dark pink ombre. There was plenty left over, but I needed the extra so that I could be intentional in my use of the fabric.

When using ombre fabric in the wings, I strongly suggest that you pre-cut the fabrics for both upper wings at the same time and both lower wings at the same time. This ensures that the wings are symmetrical and that the ombre effect is used to its full potential. I like to pin the cut fabrics in position on the paper foundations until I am ready to use them. This ensures that the correct fabric pieces are used in each position and that the colour gradient flows in the correct direction. Don't think that you have to stick to solid fabrics for this pattern. I think that the design offers some really great fussy cutting potential.

If you choose to use a directional print for borders and background it may be a good idea to cut the side borders before you piece the butterfly, as this will ensure that you use the fabric as efficiently as possible. I also strongly recommend that you read the tips on working with directional prints in the Fabric Selection chapter. It may help to mark your fabric selections on the paper patterns or the Colouring Chart.

PREPARATION

Find the relevant pages in the PDF. Print the patterns full size and check the 1in square is the correct size. Note that the pattern comes in five separate pages – one for each wing (top and bottom) and one for the body. The wings are identical but in mirror image. As such, the printed diagrams can be used for both wings, or if you prefer extra diagrams are included in the PDF. Cut out the pattern pieces. Where pieces span more than a page, glue them together before starting sewing. Take time to audition and select your fabrics and to study the diagrams.

PIECING

Foundation piece the project (see Paper Piecing: Paper Piecing Process). The construction of the right and left wings is identical. Once each section is pieced, sew them together in the following order:

Upper wing: A→B. AB→C. ABC→D. ABCD→E. F→G. H→I. HI→J. HIJ→K. FG→HIJK. ABCDE→FGHIJK.

Lower wing: A→B. C→D. E→F. CD→EF. G→H. CDEF→GH. AB→CDEFGH. I→J. IJ→K. ABCDEFGH→IJK. L→M. ABCDEFGHIJK→LM.

Butterfly body: A→B→C.

Piece the butterfly sections together as follows.

- Sew upper right wing to lower right wing.

- Sew upper left wing to lower left wing.

- Sew complete right wing to body.

- Sew complete left wing to body.

QUILT ASSEMBLY

Remove the papers. Press and starch the work (see Perfecting the Technique: Finishing a Block).

From the border fabric cut two strips 4in x 30½in and two strips 10½in x 40½in. Sew the shorter strips to the sides of the block and press seams open. Sew the longer strips to the top and bottom and press open (see Quilt Assembly Diagram).

Prepare a quilt sandwich of the quilt, wadding (batting) and backing and quilt as desired (see General Techniques). The antennae were freehand quilted.

For the binding, cut five 2¼in x width of fabric strips and bind to finish (see General Techniques: Binding).

QUILT ASSEMBLY DIAGRAM

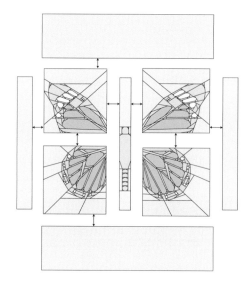

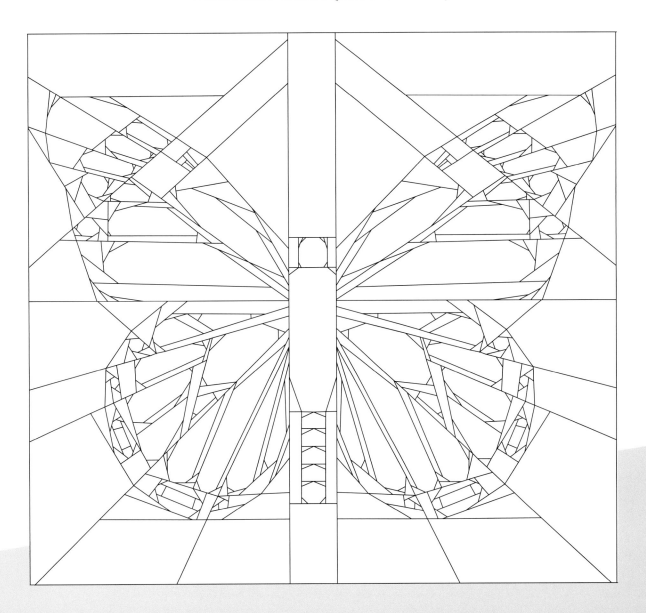

Potential Uses for this Block

MINI QUILT: This block could easily be reduced in size to 22in x 20in and used to create a beautiful mini quilt.

CUSHION: If using a 22in x 20in version of this pattern to create a square cushion, you will need to add 1½in x 22½in strips to the top and bottom of the block. Don't worry about adding borders to the left and right of the block. This will create a 22in x 22in cushion cover. See General Techniques: Making a Cushion Cover.

KING-SIZE QUILT: If you were up for a challenge, you could create four butterflies in a variety of colours and fabrics and lay them out in a grid to create a king-size quilt. Remember that you will probably want to keep the butterflies on the top of the bed and add borders to hang over the edges.

RHINO

A couple of years ago, I designed a whole safari of animals. At the time, I was keen to include a rhino, but somehow could never get the pattern to work. No matter what I did, the pattern looked clownish and wrong. I drew it, redrew it and the pattern slowly inched its way forward, but there was still something not quite right about it. Finally, help came from an unexpected source: my brother took one look at the pattern and diagnosed the issue. From that day forward, I have loved this design. The Fabric Requirements list below is for the quilt with two rhino blocks. See Potential Uses for this Block at the end of this chapter for fabric requirements for a single rhino lap quilt.

FINISHED SIZES

Block: 30in x 20in

Quilt: 40in x 40in

FABRIC REQUIREMENTS

- ⅝yd rhino body 1 fabric
- ⅝yd rhino body 2 fabric
- ¼yd black fabric
- ⅛yd each rhino 1 and rhino 2 contrasting leg fabric
- ⅛yd ear fabric
- Scrap white fabric for eye
- Scraps fabric for eye lid
- 1½yds approximately of various fabrics for background (low-volume)
- ⅛yd border 1 fabric
- ⅜yd border 2 fabric
- 48in x 48in wadding (batting)
- 48in x 48in backing fabric (2¾yds)
- ⅜yd binding fabric

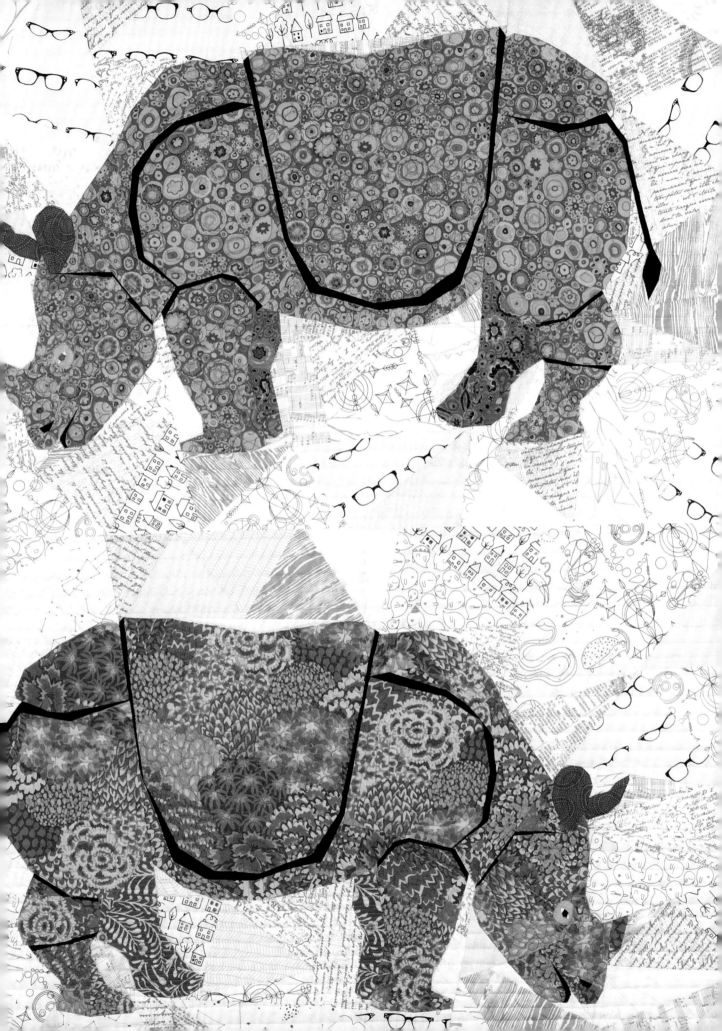

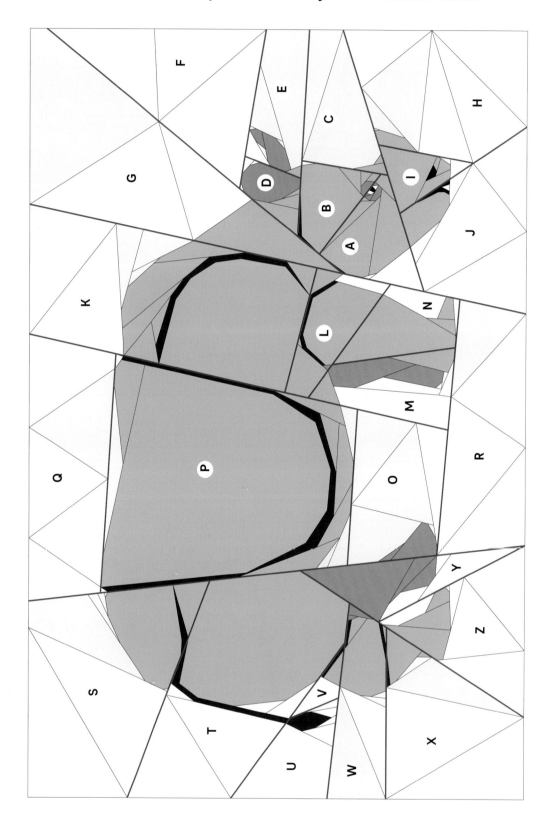

FABRIC CHOICES

I think it is important to be conscious of the effect that you want to achieve when piecing a fractured background. When I was choosing fabrics for the background of this quilt, I wanted each piece to be different from its neighbour, but I also wanted the differences to be unobtrusive and subtle. The fabrics needed to add interest and texture but not detract from the impact of the rhinos. Other options would be to create a scrappy rainbow of fabrics or to graduate colours from one shade to another, as I did in the Panda quilt. Remember to check your colour value no matter what effect you are creating.

I spent a lot of time playing with fabric choices for the rhinos themselves. In the end I chose to use a single print for the majority of the beast. If you prefer, you could use different fabrics for the different shells of the rhino's armour. You could use the same colour for all the bits of armour, but in different textures, or add an extra dimension with the careful use of lighter and darker shades.

To me, the relatively large size of the rhino welcomes a large- to medium-scale print, but be sure to choose a print that does not overwhelm the pattern by containing too much high-contrast detail.

You could keep things clean with a simple, blender-style print for the rhino. Or if you were up for a bit of fun, I think the pattern offers great potential for wonderful fussy cuts in the different areas of the armour – maybe he could have a small bird piggybacking on his rump or a large flower centred on his flank. Have fun and experiment with your fabrics.

PREPARATION

Find the relevant pages in the PDF. The patterns have been provided in two pages in the PDF, one file with the right-facing rhino and one with the left-facing rhino. Diagrams for the left-facing rhino are included in the book pages. They may be used to assist with the piecing of either rhino, but if you prefer you can find diagrams for the right-facing rhino in the PDF. Choose the rhino that you wish to sew. Print the patterns and check the 1in square is the correct size. Cut out the pattern pieces and glue them together where necessary.

Take the time to plan your fabric placement by referring to the diagrams, colouring in the Colouring Chart and writing notes on your pattern pieces. Pay special attention to the tiny pieces in the fractured background. I generally like to hide them and to make it appear as if all the pattern pieces are the same size. Do this by using the same fabric for adjacent small pieces. Be aware though that the most suitable adjacent fabric may be on a different paper template.

I personally find it easier to sew one rhino and then the other (especially when the rhinos are facing in opposite directions and I am using different fabrics for each one), but work in the way that suits you. Whatever you do, be sure not to confuse the templates of the right-facing and left-facing rhinos.

PIECING

Foundation piece the project (see Paper Piecing: Paper Piecing Process).

Once each section is pieced, sew them together in the following order:

A→B. AB→C. D→E. ABC→DE. ABCDE→F. ABCDEF→G. H→I. HI→J. ABCDEFG→HIJ. K→L. M→N. KL→MN. O→P. OP→Q. KLMN→OPQ. KLMNOPQ→R. S→T. U→V. ST→UV. W→X. STUV→WX. Y→Z. STUVWX→YZ. KLMNOPQR→STUVWXYZ. ABCDEFGHIJ→KLMNOPQRSTUVWXYZ.

QUILT ASSEMBLY

Remove the papers. Press and starch the work (see Perfecting the Technique: Finishing a Block).

Follow the Quilt Assembly Diagram, sewing the two rhino blocks together first. From border 1 fabric, cut two strips 1¼in x 40½in. From border 2 fabric, cut two strips 5in x 40½in. Sew the narrow strips to the right and left sides of the quilt. Press seams open. Sew the wider strips to the right and left sides and press open.

Prepare a quilt sandwich of the quilt, wadding (batting) and backing and quilt as desired (see General Techniques).

For the binding, cut five 2¼in x width of fabric strips and bind to finish (see General Techniques: Binding).

COLOURING CHART (REVERSE VIEW)

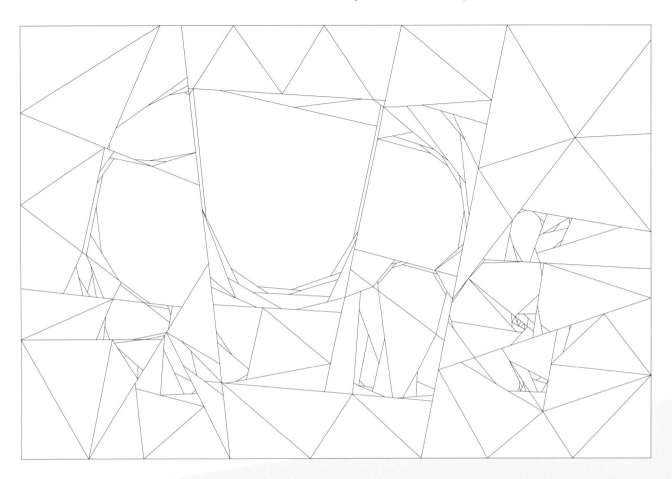

QUILT ASSEMBLY DIAGRAM

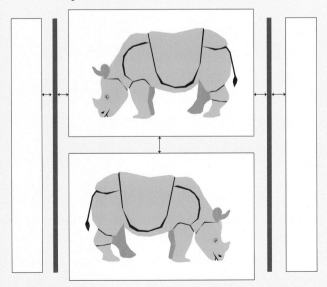

Potential Uses for this Block

LARGER QUILT: For those who like their patterns big, this pattern would be suitable to be increased in size. I would not recommend decreasing the size of the pattern, as the pieces around the eye would be too small to work with.

SINGLE RHINO LAP QUILT: If you wish to create a single rhino quilt, the pattern can be squared up by adding 5½in x 30½in borders to the top and bottom of the block. For a single rhino block you will need: ⅝yd rhino body fabric, ⅛yd black fabric, ⅛yd contrasting leg fabric, ⅛yd ear fabric, scrap of white for eye, scraps of fabric for eye lids, 1⅛yds background fabric (low-volume), ⅜yd border fabric, 38in x 28in backing fabric and wadding (batting), ¼yd binding fabric.

NIGHT OWL

I often find that a single spark of inspiration leads in many different directions and a single design idea can result in a series of designs. A couple of years ago I ran a quilt-along on my blog, which consisted of a series of flying bird silhouettes. I really wanted one of the birds to be an owl, but the pattern didn't work as a silhouette. Without the eye detail, the flying owl looked wrong, like a badly designed bird with a lumpy head! I was incredibly disappointed, as I really wanted to include a flying owl pattern, but I also wanted to do justice to the design. To me, the most important feature of an owl is the large, dramatic eyes. I let the idea simmer away at the back of my mind, and when the opportunity arose to design a flight-themed quilt for a New Zealand travelling quilt exhibition, I immediately knew what the subject would be.

FINISHED SIZES

Block: 50in x 50in

Quilt: 50in x 50in

FABRIC REQUIREMENTS

- 3yds background fabric
- Approximately eleven fat quarters or a selection of large fabric scraps
- 58in x 58in wadding (batting)
- 58in x 58in backing fabric (3¼yds)
- ½yd binding fabric

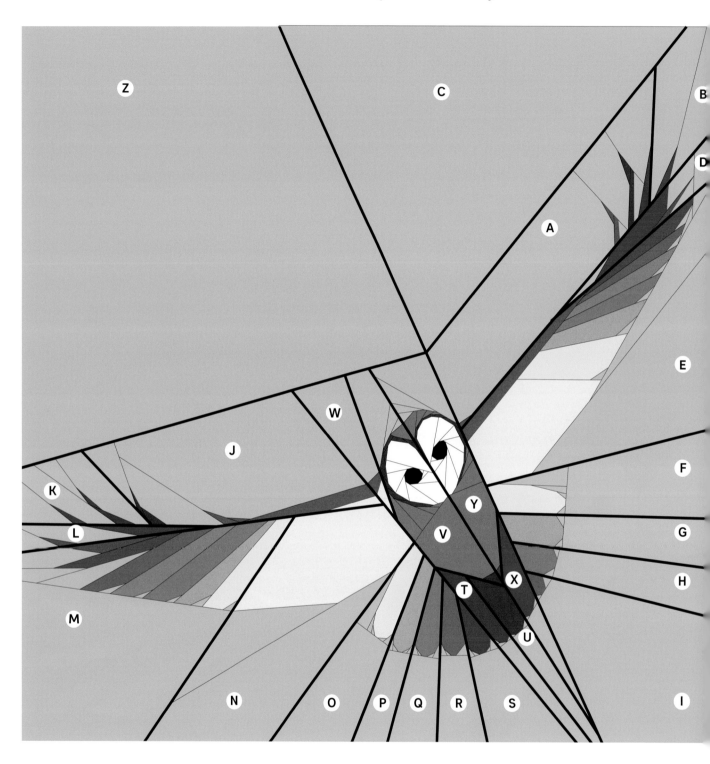

FABRIC CHOICES

This pattern allows for different interpretations – see Fabric Selection: Pattern Guidance for examples of three colour versions you might use. I chose to use ombre fabrics and to keep the fabrics simple and modern. I love the way that the ombres give depth and personality. The owl seems to be swooping out of the quilt at you. I know many Harry Potter fans see this owl as Hedwig and want to make a snowy owl version. I can't wait to see this. Pale tone-on-tone fabrics and subtle low-volume fabrics could lead to a beautiful snowy owl.

There is also the possibility of using blender-style fabrics for the owl. You might choose to use realistic brown shades, or bright and fun colours – the choice is yours. To me, half the fun of this kind of quilt is finding the fabrics that represent the textures to be depicted.

When selecting fabrics, please bear in mind that it is difficult to predict fabric usage for paper piecing. If you tend to be wasteful in your piecing, you may wish to increase the fabric requirements. If you are very precise, you may find the amounts a bit generous. I chose to use a variety of colours for the feathers, but you may prefer a subtler approach with fewer colours, in which case you will probably need less fabric.

PREPARATION

Find the relevant pages in the PDF. Print the patterns full size and check the 1in square is the correct size. Cut out the pattern pieces. This owl design has some large-scale templates that can be difficult to manipulate. I strongly recommend that you assemble each template as you are sewing. This is especially relevant for templates E and M. In each case, sew the wing feathers before completing the negative space area of the template. Templates C and Z each consist of a single large fabric piece. I recommend that you press the fabric, pin it to the paper foundation and use large tacking (basting) stitches in the seam allowance to anchor the fabric to the paper. You can then treat these pieces as you would any other pieced paper foundation, although you will probably want to unpick the tacking (basting) before you remove the paper. See Perfecting the Technique: Working with Large Fabric Pieces. Take time to select your fabrics and to study the diagrams.

PIECING

Foundation piece the sections of the project (see Paper Piecing: Paper Piecing Process).

Once each section is pieced, sew them together in the following order:

A→B. AB→C. D→E. ABC→DE. F→G. FG→H. FGH→I. ABCDE→FGHI. J→K. JK→L. M→N. MN→O. MNO→P. MNOP→Q. MNOPQ→R. MNOPQR→S. JKL→MNOPQRS. T→U. TU→V. TUV→W. JKLMNOPQRS→TUVW. X→Y. JKLMNOPQRSTUVW→XY. JKLMNOPQRSTUVWXY→Z. ABCDEFGHI→JKLMNOPQRSTUVWXYZ.

When sewing JKLMNOPQRSTUVW to XY, take extra care around pieces Y19 and V11. These pieces are sewn on a very acute angle and if the two paper pieces are sewn together carelessly, the raw edges of the seam allowance can peek through. In order to avoid this happening, ensure that the tips of Y19 and V11 that extend into the seam allowance are not cut too short. When sewing the papers together at this point, it is important that you work as accurately as possible and sew carefully along the printed lines – $\frac{1}{16}$in–$\frac{1}{8}$in deviation from the printed line can make a big difference. Be sure that you tack (baste) the seam before sewing it properly and sew slowly, as the seam is a dense one. It may be necessary to get hold of the tip that extends into the seam allowance of pieces Y19 and V11 and gently pull them back away from the seam. Once this seam has been sewn, press it open, to help distribute the bulk and make it less difficult to quilt.

QUILT ASSEMBLY

Remove the papers. Press and starch the work (see Perfecting the Technique: Finishing a Block).

Prepare a quilt sandwich of the quilt, wadding (batting) and backing (see General Techniques). Cut the backing fabric in half, into two pieces 58½in long. Remove selvedges and sew the two pieces together along the long edge. Press the seam open. Trim to 58in wide. Quilt as desired.

For the binding, cut six 2¼in x width of fabric strips and bind to finish (see General Techniques: Binding).

COLOURING CHART (REVERSE VIEW)

Potential Uses for this Block

MINI QUILT: This design can be reduced to a 30in square pattern, but I would not recommend going any smaller. At 30in, there is some pretty intensive piecing to be done on the face of the owl, with many small pieces.

PEACOCK

Every time I see a peacock, I rush home and attempt to design a pattern. Unfortunately, try as I may, I have not yet managed to perfect a pattern of the whole bird. I am determined to keep trying though and maybe one day I will succeed, but in the meantime I am really pleased with this depiction of a peacock's head. I love the way that this pattern has captured the poise, majesty and elegance of these beautiful birds.

FINISHED SIZES

Block: 25in x 30in

Quilt: 30in x 35in

FABRIC REQUIREMENTS

- 1yd background fabric
- ¾yd body fabric in mid blue (I used a variety of fabrics in similar shades, but a single fabric would work)
- ⅛yd black fabric
- ⅛yd white fabric
- ⅛yd grey fabric for beak
- ⅛yd light green fabric for around eye
- ⅛yd purple fabric
- ⅛yd dark blue fabric
- ⅛yd dark green fabric
- Scraps brown fabric for eye
- ½yd border fabric
- 38in x 43in wadding (batting)
- 38in x 43in backing fabric (1¼yds)
- ¼yd binding fabric

FABRIC CHOICES

My initial vision for this pattern was for it to be sewn in rich shot cotton tones of blue and green. It is still an interpretation that I think would work perfectly, but as I lived with the pattern, I realized that I wanted to use fabrics that offered more texture and mimicked feathers. Virtually all the prints I used to depict my peacock are large-scale flowers and I think they work perfectly in this context. I will admit that these fabrics represent the biggest risk that I have taken in fabric selection, but they really paid off. I love the effect that they create and can't wait to use more of these large-scale fabric designs in my sewing.

Check the colour value of your chosen fabrics before you start sewing. If you are using a large-scale print, be aware of distracting elements within the fabric design. If they are present, try to cut around them where possible or to place them strategically within your design.

For those who want to use less traditional colours but still remain realistic, you could consider sewing a white peacock – subtle shades of low-volume fabric could look stunning on this pattern.

PREPARATION

Find the relevant pages in the PDF. Print the patterns full size and check the 1in square is the correct size. Cut out the pattern pieces and glue them together where necessary.

Take time to audition and select your fabrics and to study the diagrams. It may help to mark your fabric selections on the peacock's paper foundations or on the Colouring Chart.

PIECING

Foundation piece the sections of the project (see Paper Piecing: Paper Piecing Process).

Once each section is pieced, sew the sections together in the following order:

A→B. C→D→E. AB→CDE. ABCDE→F. G→H. ABCDEF→GH. I→J. K→L→M→N→O. IJ→KLMNO. ABCDEFGH→IJKLMNO.

When sewing the sections together, pay special attention to aligning the critical join points (see Perfecting the Technique: Sewing Paper Sections Together). This pattern contains a wide range of sizes of pattern pieces – large fabric pieces that should be tacked (basted) to the paper using large stitches in the seam allowance, and also tiny pieces in the eye region, which you could give ⅛in seam allowances instead of the standard ¼in. Take your time and enjoy your sewing.

QUILT ASSEMBLY

Remove the papers. Press and starch the work (see Perfecting the Technique: Finishing a Block).

Measure the exact dimensions and cut the following border pieces – two strips 3in x 30½in and one strip 5½in x 30½in. Sew the narrow border strips to the left and right sides of the block and press seams open. Remeasure the width of the quilt. Trim the top border piece if necessary and then sew to the top of the quilt (see Quilt Assembly Diagram).

Prepare a quilt sandwich of the quilt, wadding (batting) and backing and quilt as desired (see General Techniques).

For the binding, cut four 2¼in x width of fabric strips and bind to finish (see General Techniques: Binding).

QUILT ASSEMBLY DIAGRAM

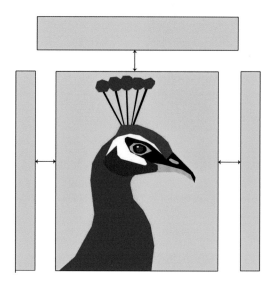

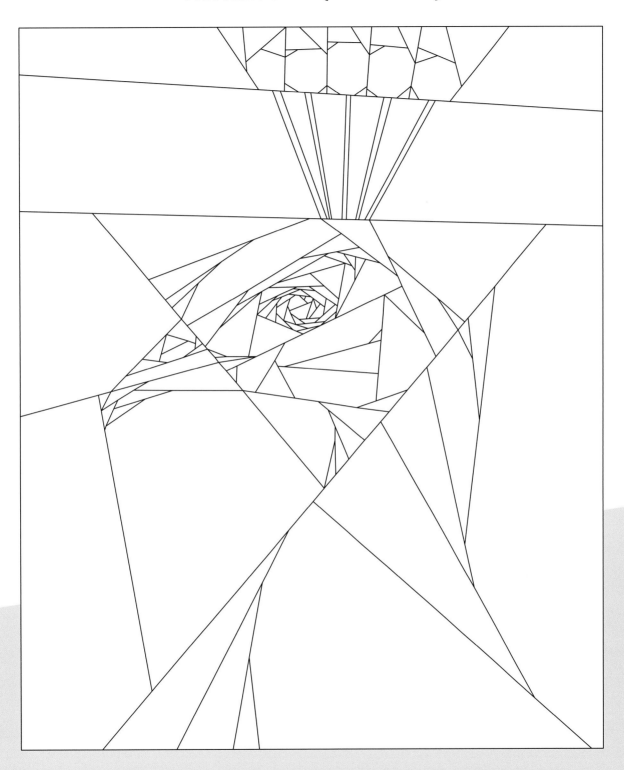

HIGHLAND COW

During a recent visit to my native Scotland, I was asked why I haven't designed more patterns of Scottish animals. I was surprised by the question as many of the bird patterns that I have designed are very personal to me and my Scottish childhood. When I took a step back though, I realized that I haven't done many Scottish animal designs and my thoughts immediately turned to Highland cows. While out and about in Scotland, it is always fun to see these docile shaggy beasts grazing in the fields. There is something comical about the way that their hair falls over their eyes while they are slowly chewing the cud.

FINISHED SIZES

Block: 20in x 20in

Quilt: 20in x 20in

FABRIC REQUIREMENTS

- ½yd background fabric

- ⅛yd horn fabric

- ¼yd lower face fabric

- About ⅜yd in total of fabric scraps for shaggy ears and forehead in a variety of different shades

- ⅛yd brown nose fabric

- Scrap pink fabric for nose

- Scrap black fabric for mouth

- Scrap grey fabric for nostril

- 24in x 24in wadding (batting)

- 24in x 24in backing fabric (¾yd)

- ¼yd binding fabric

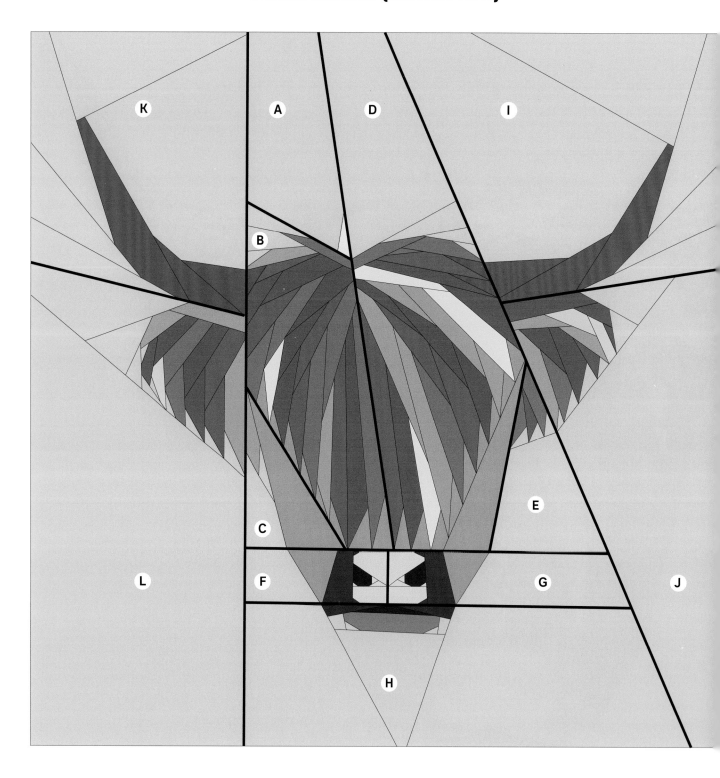

FABRIC CHOICES

This is a great block for using up small scraps of fabric. I had lots of fun choosing a selection of orange, mustard and yellow scraps from my scrap bin.

Try to ensure that the different areas of the face are distinct from each other – the scraps that are used for the shaggy ears and forehead should be clearly different from the lower part of the face. The brown part of the nose should be distinguishable from the lower face. I made this distinction by varying colour values, but you could also do it with contrast. Ensure that the horns are clearly visible against the background.

PREPARATION

Find the relevant pages in the PDF. Print the templates full size and check the 1in square is the correct size. Cut out the pattern pieces. Pieces I, J, L and M are printed on more than one page. Each must be constructed before you start sewing. Piece D also spans two pages, but it may be easier to sew sections D1 to D35 before gluing the template together. Take the time to familiarize yourself with the pattern by colouring in the Colouring Chart, and/or writing fabric choice notes on the pattern pieces.

PIECING

Foundation piece the sections of the project (see Paper Piecing: Paper Piecing Process).

Once each section is pieced, sew them together in the following order:

A→B. AB→C. D→E. ABC→DE. F→G. ABCDE→FG. ABCDEFG→H. I→J. ABCDEFGH→IJ. K→L. ABCDEFGHIJ→KL.

The central seam of this quilt (joining ABC and DE) can become very bulky at the point where all the hair converges. In order to spread the bulk, I recommend pressing the seam open. You could also press open the side seams that join the ears to the head.

QUILT ASSEMBLY

Remove the papers. Press and starch the work (see Perfecting the Technique: Finishing a Block).

Prepare a quilt sandwich of the quilt, wadding (batting) and backing and quilt as desired (see General Techniques).

For the binding, cut three 2¼in x width of fabric strips and bind to finish (see General Techniques: Binding).

COLOURING CHART (REVERSE VIEW)

Potential Uses for this Block

CUSHION: When using a pictorial block to create a cushion, I generally like to add a small border. By so doing, the image is kept away from the edges of the cushion, which stops it from being distorted by the curve of the cushion. Border strips cut 2in wide would work well for this pattern, to create a cushion to fit a 24in cushion insert. See General Techniques: Making a Cushion Cover.

QUILT: I think it would be fun to create a quilt with at least four repeats of this pattern in different colours. Why not use scraps of different colours to depict each Highland cow?

This pattern could be increased in size, but could become tricky if enlarged too much.

TIGER

This pattern was designed for my son. At the age of six he is too old for cute animals and needs something fierce and dangerous. To me, it feels as if the tiger is stalking through long grass, silently creeping up on his prey, but perhaps he is really standing guard and protecting the body asleep under the quilt. Those eyes convey so much emotion, but what are they really saying? The pattern for the tiger is split into two halves (top and bottom), each measuring 30in x 20in.

FINISHED SIZES

Block: 30in x 40in

Quilt: 40in x 50in

FABRIC REQUIREMENTS

- 1½yds background fabric
- ¼yd orange 1 fabric for face
- ⅜yd orange 2 fabric for back legs and tail
- ⅜yd orange 3 fabric for front legs and hump
- ⅜yd black fabric
- ⅛yd white fabric
- Scraps green fabric for eyes
- Scraps pink fabric for ear and nose
- ¾yd border fabric
- 48in x 58in wadding (batting)
- 48in x 58in backing fabric (2¾yds)
- ⅜yd binding fabric

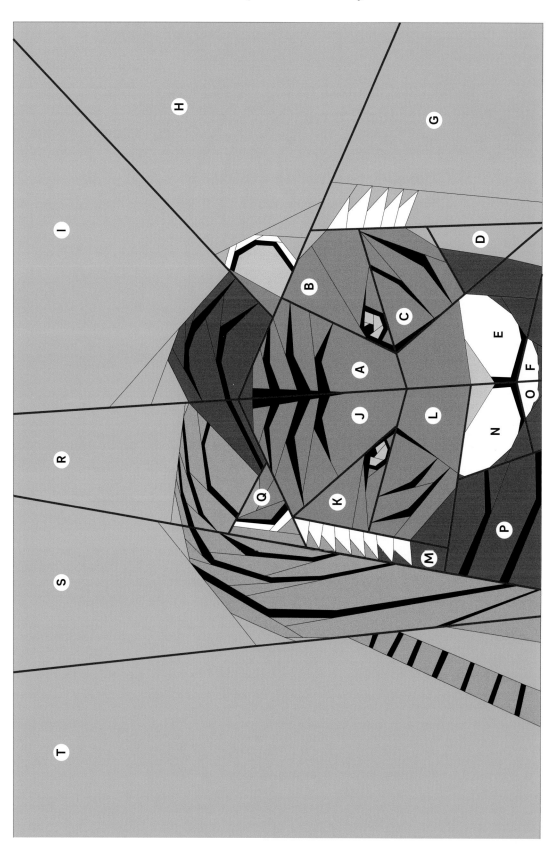

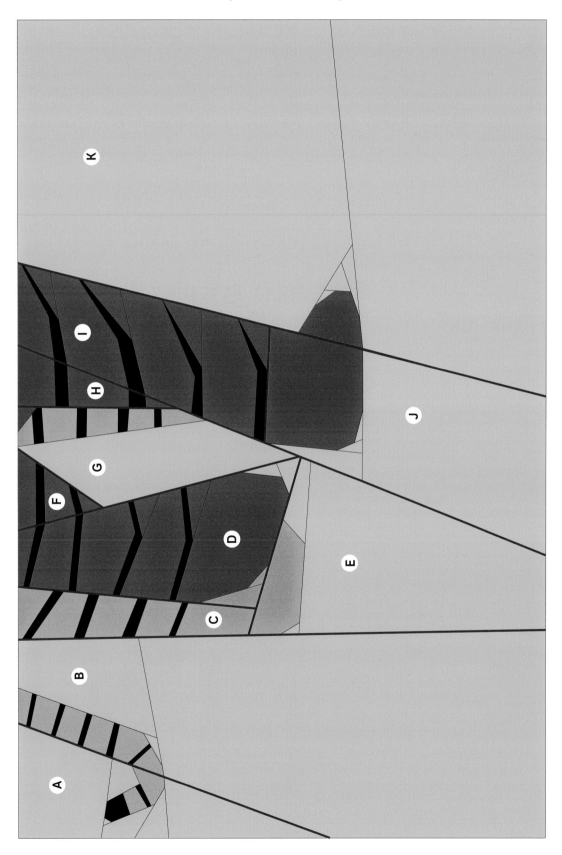

FABRIC CHOICES

This tiger has three distinct bands of orange colour and it's important that they can each be distinguished from each other. Really take the time to think about your fabric choices before you start sewing. There is a lot of sewing involved in this tiger and it would be a real shame to go to all the trouble of sewing it, only to be disappointed that some details don't show up.

For advice on choosing fabrics that can be distinguished from one another, refer to Fabric Selection: Colour Value.

If you are not a fan of orange tones, you could consider making a white tiger.

PREPARATION

Find the relevant pages in the PDF. Print the templates full size and check the 1in square is the correct size. The pattern has been constructed as two blocks. To avoid confusion, ensure that you keep the pieces of the two blocks separate and prepare the pattern pieces for one block at a time. There is significantly more work involved in sewing the top block than the bottom block. Cut out the pattern pieces. Paper templates G, H, I, R, S and T of the upper body are pieces that span more than one page. Pieces G and R can each be glued together before being sewn. Piece H: sew pieces 1 to 13 before gluing the remainder of the template together Piece I: sew pieces 1 to 16 before gluing the remainder of the template together. Piece S spans three pages: glue the first two pieces together and sew pieces 1 to 27 and then construct the remainder of the template. Piece T: sew pieces 1 to 17 and then construct the remainder of the template.

PIECING

Foundation piece the sections of the project (see Paper Piecing: Paper Piecing Process).

Once each section is pieced, sew them together in the following order. (For tips on accurately sewing sections together, see Perfecting the Technique: Sewing Paper Sections Together.)

Upper body: A→B. C→D. CD→E. CDE→F. AB→CDEF. ABCDEF→G. H→I. ABCDEFG→HI. J→K. JK→L. JKL→M. N→O. NO→P. JKLM→NOP. Q→R. JKLMNOP→QR. JKLMNOPQR→S. JKLMNOPQRS→T ABCDEFGHI→JKLMNOPQRST.

Lower body: A→B. C→D. CD→E. AB→CDE. F→G→H. ABCDE→FGH. I→J. IJ→K. ABCDEFGH→IJK.

Once the upper body and the lower body are assembled, match up the critical joining points and sew the two halves together.

QUILT ASSEMBLY

Remove the papers, taking care to remove the tiny pieces from the thin stripes and small pieces. Press and starch the work (see Perfecting the Technique: Finishing a Block).

For the border cut four strips each 5½in x 40½in. Sew a border strip to the right and left sides of the quilt and press seams open (see Quilt Assembly Diagram). Check the measurements of the top and bottom borders before sewing these final border strips in place. See General Techniques: Borders, for advice on adding borders properly.

Prepare a quilt sandwich of the quilt, wadding (batting) and backing and quilt as desired (see General Techniques).

For the binding, cut five 2¼in x width of fabric strips and bind to finish (see General Techniques: Binding).

QUILT ASSEMBLY DIAGRAM

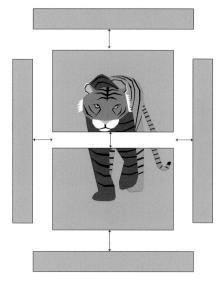

CLYDESDALE HORSE

I am not a horse rider and I know nothing about horses, but it doesn't take an expert to recognize the outstanding strength, grace, presence and power of a Clydesdale horse. I have vivid childhood memories of seeing these massive work horses when my family visited the Highland Show in Scotland. There are few things more impressive than seeing these horses kitted out in their show finery, with elaborate bridles and ribbons adorning their braided manes. When I sat down to design a horse pattern, I knew that it had to be a magnificent Clydesdale.

FINISHED SIZES

Block: 21in x 14in

Quilt: 21in x 14in

FABRIC REQUIREMENTS

- ½yd background fabric
- ¼yd horse fabric
- ⅛yd white fabric
- ⅛yd back legs fabric
- Scrap black fabric for eye
- 25in x 18in wadding (batting)
- 25in x 18in backing fabric (½yd)
- ⅛yd binding fabric

COLOUR DIAGRAM (REVERSE VIEW)

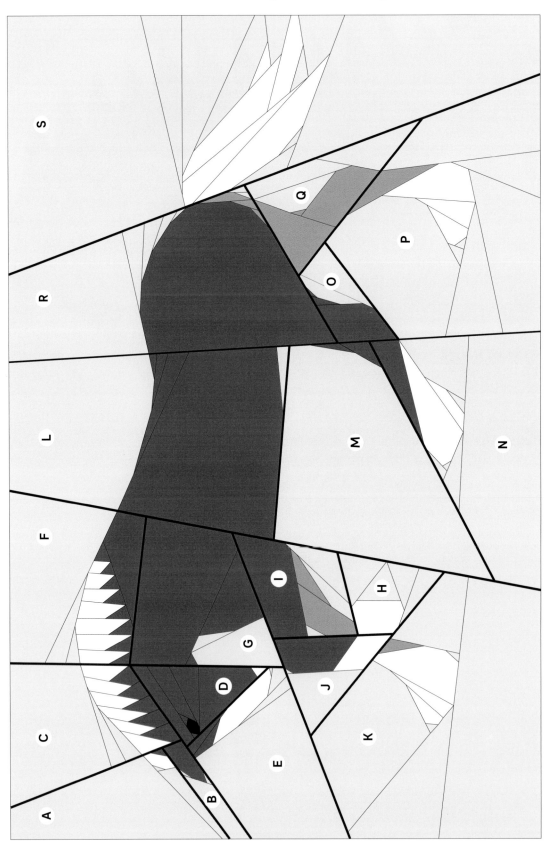

FABRIC CHOICES

I sewed this quilt using a fairly limited colour palette, but there is nothing to stop you from adding a larger variety of shades or colours. There are many different directions that you could take the pattern in: one suggestion would be to use fabrics in a single colour, but with different textures for the horse's body.

You may notice that there are yellow details in the print that I used for the body of the horse. As the background is a similar shade of yellow, I was careful to mainly cut around this colour and avoided it where possible. Where I did use yellow, I carefully kept it away from the junction with the yellow background as I did not want it to 'eat' into the horse's silhouette and thus detract from the clean outline of the horse.

I spent a lot of time choosing the fabrics for this mini quilt. The main challenge was ensuring that there was enough of a difference in colour value between the three main fabrics – the background, the body of the horse and the white detail on the horse. I took many, many black and white photos before finally deciding that there was enough of a difference in colour value between the yellow and the white. I had slight reservations that the white in the background print would be distracting, but luckily it is subtle enough to not be a problem.

PREPARATION

Find the relevant pages in the PDF. Print the templates full size and check the 1in square is the correct size. Cut out the pattern pieces. Paper template S spans two pages. It is best to glue the template together after pieces 1 to 11 have been sewn.

Take time to audition and select your fabrics, and to study the diagrams. It may help you to mark your fabric selections on the paper foundations or the Colouring Chart.

PIECING

Foundation piece the sections of the project (see Paper Piecing: Paper Piecing Process).

This pattern contains some very small pieces. They give subtlety to the outline of the horse and detail to the pattern. Don't be intimidated by them. Some people like to reduce the seam allowance of tiny pieces to ⅛in, to minimize the build-up of bulk and make quilting easier. If you choose not to decrease the seam allowance of small pieces, make sure that you press the block well before quilting. If you find a particular seam between the sections to be very bulky, press it open. This shares the bulk on both sides of the seam and makes it easier to quilt.

Once each section is pieced, sew them together in the following order:

A→B. AB→C. D→E. ABC→DE. F→G. ABCDE→FG. H→I. HI→J. HIJ→K. ABCDEFG→HIJK. L→M→N. ABCDEFGHIJK→LMN. O→P. OP→Q. OPQ→R. OPQR→S. ABCDEFGHIJKLMN→OPQRS.

QUILT ASSEMBLY

Remove the papers. Press and starch the work (see Perfecting the Technique: Finishing a Block).

Prepare a quilt sandwich of the quilt, wadding (batting) and backing and quilt as desired (see General Techniques).

For the binding, cut two 2¼in x width of fabric strips and bind to finish (see General Techniques: Binding).

COLOURING CHART (REVERSE VIEW)

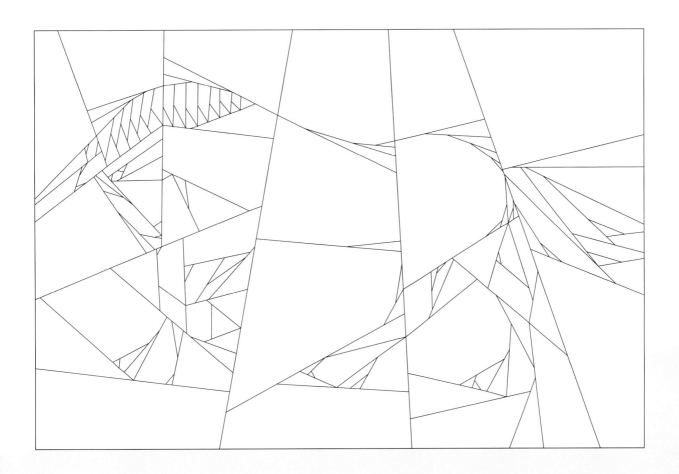

Potential Uses for this Block

TABLE RUNNER: The long, thin dimensions of this pattern make it suitable for use as a table runner. One option would be to place a single horse in the centre of the runner. Another option would be to have a row of three or four horses. I think that any table would look spectacular with a row of horses galloping along it.

CUSHION: To use this design to create a cushion, I suggest squaring the design up by adding borders 4in x 21½in to the top and bottom of the block. Further borders are not essential, but adding a 2in border around the design moves the design away from the edges. See General Techniques: Making a Cushion Cover.

LARGER QUILT: I initially intended this pattern to be a large-scale one, but for various reasons decided to sew it as a mini quilt. You can easily increase the size of the pattern to 20in x 30in. If you are feeling adventurous, try making it even bigger. I would not decrease the size of the pattern.

POLAR BEAR

The very first large-scale paper-pieced pattern that I designed was a bear. Although I love the pattern, I must admit that Big Bear is not the easiest to sew. I have learnt a lot about writing large-scale patterns since I designed him and I wanted to try a new bear design. This quilt is the result. The Norse mythological name for a polar bear is 'rider of icebergs', which I think is a great title for a quilt. It conjures up an amazing image in my head and I hope I have translated that into fabric. I love the way that the blues of the background in this mini quilt evoke images of icebergs and frozen rivers.

FINISHED SIZES

Block: 24in x 24in

Quilt: 24in x 24in

FABRIC REQUIREMENTS

- ½yd white 1 fabric
- ⅛yd white 2 fabric
- ⅛yd white 3 fabric
- ⅛yd black fabric
- Scraps grey fabric 1 for ear
- Scraps grey fabric 2 for ear
- ⅛yd pink fabric
- Fabrics in varying shades of blue (about 1yd in total)
- 28in x 28in wadding (batting)
- 28in x 28in backing fabric (¾yd)
- ¼yd binding fabric

COLOUR DIAGRAM (REVERSE VIEW)

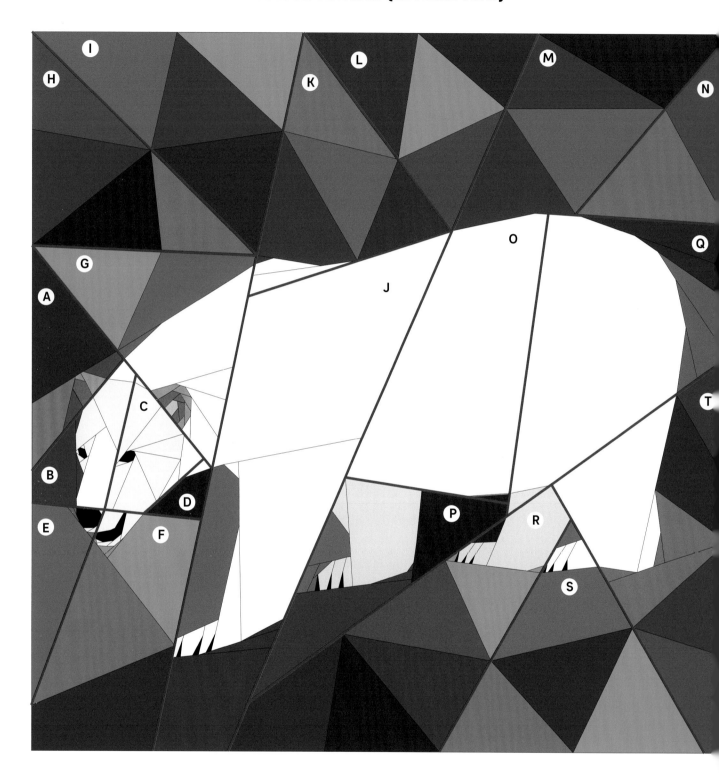

FABRIC CHOICES

At least three different shades of light-coloured fabrics are required to sew the polar bear. Be sure to take the time to choose distinguishable shades of white. While it is true that quilting can be used to help define the borders between different body parts, fabric choices should also play a role. Consider using different light-coloured fabrics such as white, cream and light grey. You may prefer to use fabrics with different types of designs – flowers in one area, cross-hatch in another and dots in another. Another alternative is to mix up solid fabrics with patterned or tone-on-tone prints. Try to choose fabrics that are distinct from each other without being too distracting. Once you have chosen your fabrics, lay them together, take a photograph, look at them, both close up and from a distance. Are you still happy with your choices?

Three separate shades of white have been specified in the Fabric Requirements, as this will allow you to define the head, body and legs from the most distant side of the body, but you can add more shades of white if you want. I like to give the nose a completely different shade and you could also make the paws a bit dirty.

One of the tricky things about having a white subject is that many of the fabrics that you may consider using in the background have white detail on them. This can easily distract from the sharp, clean outline of the bear. In my quilt, you will notice that although there are fabrics with white details in the background, none of these have been placed adjacent to the bear. Instead they have been deliberately scattered around the outside of the quilt.

Another thing to consider when choosing your background fabrics is colour value. Try not to use any fabrics that are too light as they may detract from the bear.

Although this pattern has been designed as a polar bear, there is nothing to stop you from taking a bit of creative license. Why not turn him into a black bear hiding in the bushes or a brown bear strolling over grasslands?

PREPARATION

Find the relevant pages in the PDF. Print the patterns full size and check the 1in square is the correct size. Cut out the pattern pieces. Where templates span more than one page, they must be glued together before sewing begins.

Although I do not necessarily plan out every single detail of my quilts before I start sewing, I think that it pays to consider fabric placement for the fractured background. If there are tiny fabric pieces there, I suggest disguising their existence by using the same fabric as the adjacent piece. You can use the Colouring Chart and the paper patterns to write notes to yourself, especially as the most suitable adjacent fabric may not be on the same pattern template.

PIECING

Foundation piece the sections of the project (see Paper Piecing: Paper Piecing Process).

Once each section is pieced, sew them together in the following order:

A→B→C→D. E→F. ABCD→EF. ABCDEF→G. H→I. ABCDEFG→HI. J→K→L. ABCDEFGHI→JKL. M→N. O→P. OP→Q. MN→OPQ. R→S. RS→T. MNOPQ→RST. ABCDEFGHIJKL→MNOPQRST.

Remember to pay attention to the critical join points so that the bear has a nice, neat outline.

QUILT ASSEMBLY

Remove the papers. Press and starch the work (see Perfecting the Technique: Finishing a Block).

Prepare a quilt sandwich of the quilt, wadding (batting) and backing and quilt as desired (see General Techniques).

For the binding, cut three 2¼in x width of fabric strips and bind to finish (see General Techniques: Binding).

COLOURING CHART (REVERSE VIEW)

Potential Uses for this Block

LARGE CUSHION: This pattern would make a wonderful outsized cushion. Although a border would not be strictly necessary, I like to add one when making a cushion from a paper-pieced animal block, as it keeps the image away from the edges and avoids distorting the image. A 2in border would be sufficient. See General Techniques: Making a Cushion Cover.

LARGER QUILT: This pattern is definitely one that could be increased in size. The number of pattern pieces involved would mean that none of them would become too large and unwieldy if enlarged. The small templates around the mouth would also become easier to sew. I think that this pattern would make a really fun baby's play quilt.

BEAR DUO: I have always thought that the Polar Bear and Panda mini quilts would make a great pair. If you want them both to be the same size, I recommend that you increase the size of the Panda rather than decreasing the size of the Polar Bear. You could make a pair of matching mini quilts/cushions, or you could combine the patterns in a single larger quilt.

HUNTED

When I was a girl, my family would spend long summer evenings in the Orkney Isles watching short-eared owls swooping low over the heather. I must admit that I didn't have the best attention span for birdwatching, but if any bird was likely to captivate and excite me, it was an owl. They caught my imagination in a way that other birds did not. I have never seen a barn owl in the wild, but I have always thought of them as the most beautiful of all the owls. When writing up this pattern, I divided it into two separate elements – the owl and the mouse. Use them individually or together, as you desire. The Fabric Requirements list below is for the quilt – see Potential Uses for this Block for fabric requirements for the owl and mouse alone.

FINISHED SIZES

Owl block: 24in x 24in

Mouse block: 12in x 6in

Quilt: 38in x 40in

FABRIC REQUIREMENTS

- 2½yds background fabric

- Approx ⅜yd various tan fabrics for owl body and upper feathers

- Approx ¾yd various light tone-on-tone or low-volume fabrics for owl face, lower feathers and legs

- ⅛yd dark brown accent fabric

- Scraps grey fabric for detail on owl face

- ⅛yd tan or grey fabric for mouse body

- ⅛yd pink fabric for mouse feet, tail, nose and ears

- Scraps black fabric for eyes

- Scraps white fabric for detail on mouse face

- 46in x 48in wadding (batting)

- 46in x 48in backing fabric (2½yds)

- ⅜yd binding fabric

COLOUR DIAGRAM (REVERSE VIEW) – MOUSE

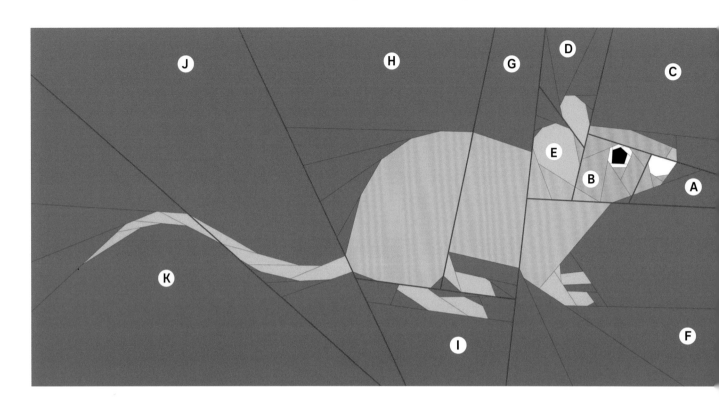

FABRIC CHOICES

I chose to use relatively realistic colours and textures for this quilt, but it would also be fun in bright and bold colours. A simple change that would make a huge difference to the overall appearance of the quilt would be to use a lighter background. Take time to audition and select your fabrics and to study the diagrams.

PREPARATION

Find the relevant pages in the PDF. Print the templates full size and check the 1in square is the correct size. Cut out the templates – some of them will need to have parts glued together. Refer to the layout diagram in the PDF to help with the construction of the pattern pieces. The owl paper template W is large and contains many small sections. I strongly suggest that you construct the template as you are sewing. Glue the first two pieces together and sew pieces 1 to 5. Glue the next part of the template and sew to piece 37. Construct the remainder of the template to sew the final piece. I also suggest that you sew pieces 1 to 7 of template U before constructing the rest of the template.

PIECING THE OWL

Foundation piece the sections of the project (see Paper Piecing: Paper Piecing Process). The challenge when piecing the owl is that some of the fabric pieces are very large and can become difficult to control. I strongly recommend that you anchor the fabric to the paper using the advice given in Perfecting the Technique: Working with Large Fabric Pieces.

The small face pieces can lead to the build-up of significant bulk, so you could trim the fabric seam allowances to around ⅛in. The seam allowance around paper sections should always remain ¼in. If you are worried about running out of fabric, sew the large sections first and then make use of your scraps as you sew the smaller sections.

Once each section is pieced, sew them together in the following order:

A→B. AB→C. ABC→D. ABCD→E. F→G. ABCDE→FG. H→I. HI→J. HIJ→K. HIJK→L. HIJKL→M. HIJKLM→N. HIJKLMN→O. HIJKLMNO→P. HIJKLMNOP→Q. ABCDEFG→HIJKLMNOPQ. R→S. RS→T. RST→U. RSTU→V. RSTUV→W. ABCDEFGHIJKLMNOPQ→RSTUVW

The small eye and face pieces mean that these seams will become bulky, so press the seam between A and B open, and also the

seam between ABC and D. There are more seams that you may choose to press open. Remember to pay particular attention to the accuracy of the joins at the critical join points.

PIECING THE MOUSE

Foundation piece the sections of the project. When piecing the eye and cheek areas, there are lots of tiny overlapping pieces. To avoid the build-up of bulk, cut fabric seam allowances smaller than ⅛in. Press seam AB open. Once each section is pieced, sew them together in the following order:

A→B. AB→C. D→E. ABC→DE. ABCDE→F. G→H. GH→I. ABCDEF→GHI. ABCDEFGHI→J. ABCDEFGHIJ→K.

QUILT ASSEMBLY

Carefully remove the papers from the blocks. Press and starch the work (see Perfecting the Technique: Finishing a Block).

If making the blocks into a complete quilt, you will need border strips. You could pre-cut these from the background fabric *before* piecing the blocks to ensure you have the correct lengths, as follows – one strip 12½in x 24½in (a), one strip 12½in x 30½in (b), two strips 2½in x 36½in (c) and one strip 2½in x 40½in (d).

With reference to the Quilt Assembly Diagram, sew the border pieces in position. Sew strip (a) to the bottom of the owl block. Sew strip (b) to the top of the mouse block. Sew the mouse unit to the left side of the owl unit. Sew strips (c) to the top and bottom of the owl and mouse unit. Sew strip (d) to the left edge of the quilt.

QUILT ASSEMBLY DIAGRAM

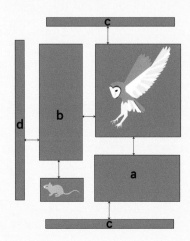

Prepare a quilt sandwich of the quilt, wadding (batting) and backing (see General Techniques). Cut the backing fabric in half, into two pieces 45in long. Remove selvedges and sew the two pieces together along the long edge. Press the seam open. Trim to 48in wide.

Quilt as desired. This is the only quilt in the book that I quilted myself on my domestic sewing machine. I stitched in the ditch around the mouse and the owl and sewed gently curved parallel lines in the background using a walking foot. I then free-motion quilted feather details. As a finishing touch, I added a few diagonal lines radiating from the owl's claws towards the mouse. I quilted these lines using thicker thread in a contrasting colour. If you are not confident in your quilting ability, straight line quilting could be effective. Consider the direction that the straight lines should run.

For the binding, cut four 2¼in x width of fabric strips and bind to finish (see General Techniques: Binding). I chose to use the same fabric for my binding as for the background. To me, this quilt didn't need a frame – it felt wrong to 'cage' a wildlife scene.

COLOURING CHART (REVERSE VIEW) – OWL

COLOURING CHART (REVERSE VIEW) – MOUSE

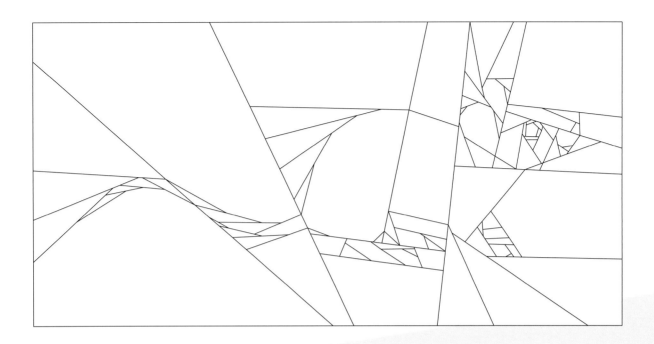

Potential Uses for this Block

The fun thing about this quilt is that it consists of two separate blocks, both of which can easily be used individually. I know that my daughter would adore a zipper pouch or cushion made with the mouse pattern.

OWL MINI QUILT: The barn owl would make a great mini quilt on its own. You will need: 1⅝yds background fabric, scraps of various tan fabrics (⅜yd total), scraps of various light low-volume, tone-on-tone fabrics (¾yd total), ⅛yd dark brown accent fabric, scraps black fabric for the eye, scraps grey fabric for the face, 28in x 28in backing fabric and wadding (batting), ¼yd binding fabric.

MOUSE MINI QUILT: For the mouse alone you will need: ¼yd background fabric, ⅛yd tan fabric for body and head (you may choose to use a different shade for the head), scrap of black for the eye, scraps of white for the eye and snout, ⅛yd pink for tail, nose, ears and feet, 16in x 10in backing fabric and wadding (batting), ⅛yd binding fabric.

HOWL

I can't remember exactly when I decided to design a wolf quilt, but it's an idea that I have been working on for a while. My initial attempts depicted a wolf's face but try as I might, I couldn't get the pattern to work. It took a lot of play and extensive research for me to create a pattern that I loved. Some may say that its simple aesthetic is different to the other quilts in this book, but to me it represents a stage in the evolution of my quilt designs. The fabric requirements here are for the Howl quilt – see Potential Uses for this Block for the fabric requirements for a lone wolf mini quilt.

FINISHED SIZES

Block: 20in x 20in

Quilt: 60in x 80in

FABRIC REQUIREMENTS

- 2yds black fabric

- Red-toned fabrics for moon, about sixteen 10in squares (see Fabric Choices)

- Blue-toned fabrics for moon, about sixteen 10in squares (see Fabric Choices)

- 2¼yds border fabric

- 68in x 88in wadding (batting)

- 68in x 88in backing fabric (5yds)

- ⅝yd binding fabric

COLOUR DIAGRAM (REVERSE VIEW)

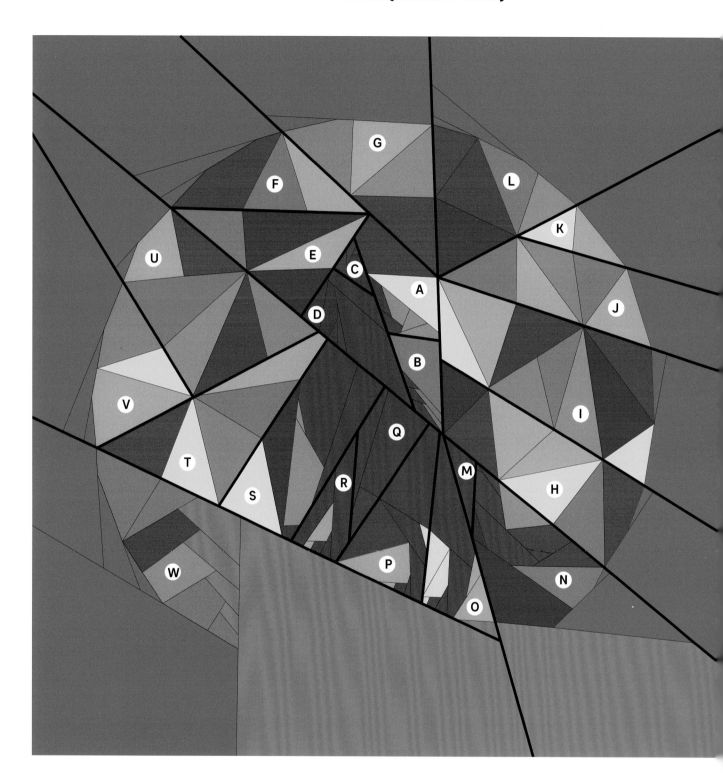

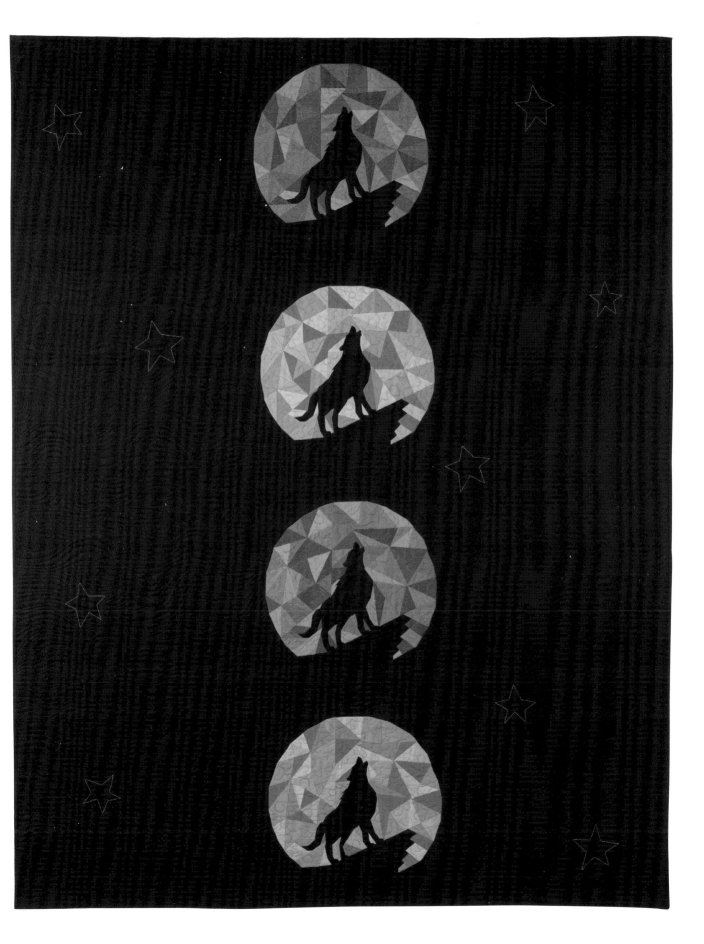

FABRIC CHOICES

Fabric quantities are difficult to predict with foundation piecing. For this design I used Oakshott cottons for the moons – two fat eighth bundles (a red-toned and a blue-toned), each containing sixteen colours. All of these were cut in half before piecing, resulting in fabric pieces about 10in x 13½in. I only used these half pieces in my quilt, and had plenty of scraps left over. No extra red or blue fabric was necessary. Fabric requirements for a single wolf block are given in Potential Uses for this Block.

There are various ways in which you can interpret this design. I used the same fabric for the sky, wolf and rocky crag, but I also love the idea of using different fabrics for each of these three elements, or perhaps using the same fabrics for the wolf and the crag with a different shade for the sky. For this you will require 1yd sky background fabric, ½yd wolf fabric, ⅝yd rocky crag fabric as well as 2¼yds border fabric. The moon fabric requirements remain unchanged.

Remember to consider colour value when choosing your fabrics. Try to use mid- or light-toned fabrics for the moon to ensure that they do not distract from the pattern outlines. Before I started piecing, I laid all of the colour fabrics on the black background, took a photo and applied a black and white filter. I discovered that three of the blue tones were too dark and disappeared against the black background, but all the red tones were safe to use.

Think creatively in terms of the colours that you wish to use. I chose to have my wolf standing in front of blood red and blue moons, but there are endless other possibilities. I used low-volume fabrics for the moon on one of my test versions of this quilt and I loved it. Why stick to realistic colours? This would be a really fun quilt in bright colours.

PREPARATION

Find the relevant pages in the PDF. Print the templates full size and check the 1in square is the correct size. Cut out the pattern pieces. Pattern templates are provided for a single wolf. If you wish to sew more, you will need to print multiple copies. Pieces I and H should be glued together before they are sewn. Glue piece W together only after pieces 1 to 13 have been sewn.

With this pattern, I think the majority of the fabric planning will be reserved for fabric placement within the fractured moon. When planning the fabrics for the moon, pay attention to the way that they are laid out. In general, try not to place the same fabrics next to each other. That said, if you place the same fabric on either side of a paper join, it can serve to hide the paper sections to make it harder for people to guess how the block has been constructed. When looking at the fabric pieces for the moon, you will notice that the majority of the sections are roughly uniform in size, but that there are a number of smaller pieces close in to the wolf itself. I like to be intentional in my fabric placement when sewing these small pieces. By using the same fabrics on some of these small pieces, it is possible to disguise that so many small pieces are present. For example, I used the same fabrics for pieces A1, A4 and A5. I also used the same fabrics for B2, B4 and B6.

Take time to audition and select your fabrics, and to study the diagrams. You could mark the pattern pieces or the Colouring Chart with letters to help with fabric placement. For example, mark pieces B for the wolf, crag and background sky, and leave the moon pieces unmarked.

PIECING

Foundation piece the sections of the project (see Paper Piecing: Paper Piecing Process).

When sewing the complete quilt, I prefer to sew one complete wolf block and then move on to the next one. It makes me feel as if I am making real progress and I enjoy having clear benchmarks that show how far I still have to go. That said, it is far more methodical to cut and sew all four wolves at the same time. Work in the way that suits your own style.

Once each section is pieced, sew them together in the following order:

A→B. C→D. AB→CD. E→F. ABCD→EF. ABCDEF→G. H→I. HI→J. HIJ→K. HIJK→L. ABCDEFG→HIJKL. M→N. O→P. Q→R. OP→QR. OPQR→S. OPQRS→T. U→V. OPQRST→UV. OPQRSTUV→W. MN→OPQRSTUVW. ABCDEFGHIJKL→MNOPQRSTUVW.

There are a lot of critical join points around the edge of the moon. Take the time to pin and tack (baste) these seams, taking care to make the joins as accurate as possible.

QUILT ASSEMBLY

Remove the papers. Press and starch the work (see Perfecting the Technique: Finishing a Block).

Lay the wolf blocks out in a column. If the moons in your quilt are sewn with different colours, ensure that you are happy with the distribution of colour. Sew the column of blocks together in the chosen order (see Quilt Assembly Diagram).

To add the borders, take the 2¼yds piece of fabric and cut it in half lengthwise. The cut should be parallel to the selvedges. Trim off the selvedges and create two pieces 20½in x 80½in. Carefully pin the first border to the column of wolves, matching the centre point, the ends and the quarter marks. Fill the gaps with further pins, ensuring that the fabric is evenly distributed. Sew the seam using a ¼in seam allowance and press the seam open. Repeat this process to attach the second border.

Prepare a quilt sandwich of the quilt, wadding (batting) and backing (see General Techniques). Cut the backing fabric in half, into two pieces 90in long. Remove selvedges and sew the two pieces together along the long edge. Press the seam open. Trim to 68in wide. Quilt as desired.

For the binding, cut eight 2¼in x width of fabric strips and bind to finish (see General Techniques: Binding).

QUILT ASSEMBLY DIAGRAM

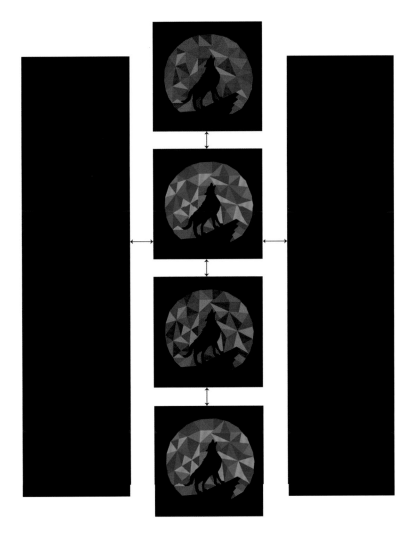

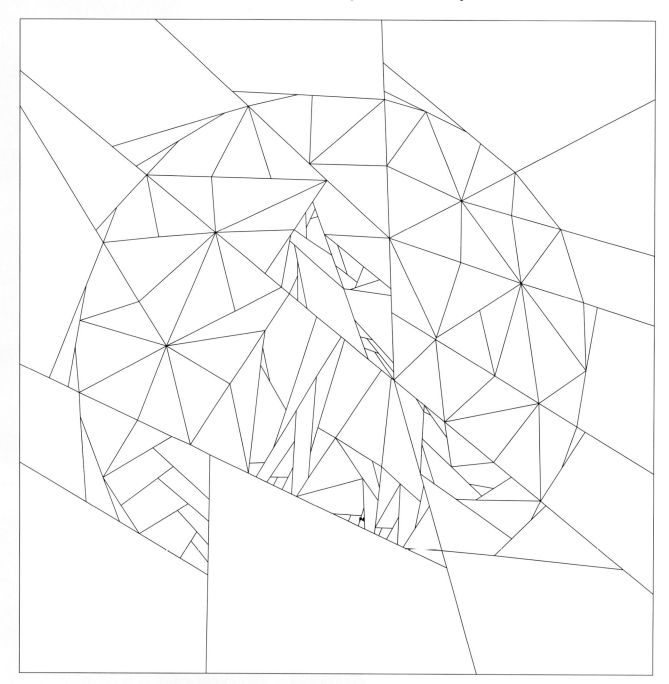

Potential Uses for this Block

LONE WOLF MINI QUILT: A single version of the wolf block could easily be used as a mini quilt. For this you would need ½yd sky background fabric, ⅛yd wolf fabric, ⅛yd rocky crag fabric, a variety of scraps for the moon and suitable amounts of backing, wadding (batting) and binding fabrics.

LONE WOLF CUSHION: This design could be used to create a 20in cushion cover. Borders could be added if you prefer a larger cushion, but this is not essential. See General Techniques: Making a Cushion Cover.

LARGER QUILT: My initial vision for this quilt was for it to consist of a single very large-scale block with borders. For various reasons, I changed my mind and sewed a smaller version, but the idea is still buzzing around at the back of my head.

ALTERNATIVE QUILT TOPS: There are many different ways in which four wolf blocks could be laid out, depending upon your own design aesthetic and the size of quilt that you want to create. I seriously played with the idea of a horizontal line of wolves across the lower half of a queen-size quilt. I also considered a smaller quilt top with the blocks arranged in a grid.

SWAN

I was listening to the Swan from the *Carnival of the Animals* by Saint-Saëns while I worked on this pattern. It is a beautiful tune that I played on the cello when I was younger. I wanted my pattern to carry the same gentle elegance and layers of meaning. I love the idea of the swan being reflected in still waters. The Fabric Requirements list below is for the quilt – see Potential Uses for this Block for fabric requirements for a single swan with border.

FINISHED SIZES

Swan block: 30in x 20in

Quilt: 50in x 60in

FABRIC REQUIREMENTS

- 1¼yds background 1 fabric
- 1¼yds background 2 fabric
- 2yds white low-volume, tone-on-tone fabric
- ⅛yd black fabric
- ⅛yd orange fabric
- 1yd border 1 fabric
- 1yd border 2 fabric
- 58in x 68in wadding (batting)
- 58in x 68in backing fabric (3¼yds)
- ½yd single-colour binding fabric or ¼yd each of two colours

FABRIC CHOICES

This pattern really excites me: the multiple possibilities for its interpretation have my mind whirring and I can't help but think that if I can think of so many options, you guys will come up with even more amazing interpretations. I chose to interpret this pattern as a single swan reflected in the water and as a result I wanted to make the distinction between the colour of the water and the colour of the sky. A different possibility would be to use a single fabric for the background of the whole quilt.

It was also important to me to make a distinction between the real swan and the reflected one, so I differentiated them by using a combination of solid and tone-on-tone fabrics for one swan and carefully chosen low-volume fabrics for the other. You may prefer to accurately mirror the fabric placement in the two swans.

Not all swans are white, so you could consider sewing a single black swan or a quilt with one black swan and one white one. Why not go a step further and create a largely monochrome quilt – a white swan on a black/dark grey background, a black swan on a white background with the only flash of colour being the orange of the beak?

PREPARATION

Find the relevant pages in the PDF. Print the templates full size and check the 1in square is the correct size. Cut out the pattern pieces. The two swans on this quilt are in mirror image to each other. The Colour Diagram of the right-facing swan is printed in the book, while the mirror image diagrams are in the PDF.

A number of pattern pieces span more than one page and must be glued together. Pieces F, G, K, L, N and O can be constructed before sewing. Sew pieces D1 to D4 before gluing template D together. Glue the lower two papers of template E together, sew pieces E1 to E16 before gluing the final piece of the template. Sew pieces M1 to M16 then construct the template and sew the remaining pieces.

If you are sewing two swans, and choose to use different fabrics for each bird, ensure that you do not muddle up the pattern pieces of the two swans. Before you sew a single stitch, familiarize yourself with the pattern. Do this by referring to the Colour Diagram (and the Number Diagram in the PDF). Use colouring pencils to shade the Colouring Chart in tones representing the fabrics that you intend to use. Try to think about which feathers belong to the front wing and which belong to the

back wing. If you wish, you could write fabric placement notes on the pattern pieces. For example, mark a W for white, B for black and O for orange. The remaining, unmarked pieces would then be background.

PIECING

Foundation piece the sections of the project (see Paper Piecing: Paper Piecing Process).

Once each section is pieced, sew them together in the following order:

A→B. C→D. AB→CD. ABCD→E. F→G. ABCDE→FG. H→I. J→K→L. HI→JKL. HIJKL→M. HIJKLM→N. HIJKLMN→O. ABCDEFG→HIJKLMNO.

QUILT ASSEMBLY

Remove the papers. Press and starch the work (see Perfecting the Technique: Finishing a Block).

For the quilt, with reference to the Quilt Assembly Diagram, cut three border strips in background fabric 1 and three strips in background fabric 2, each 30½in x 10½in. Measure the quilt width to ensure that the border will be the correct length (see General Techniques: Borders). If necessary, trim the length of the first border piece so it is the same as the measurement just taken. Sew the border to the top of the block and press the seam open.

Measure the height of the swan block with border attached and if necessary trim the length of the two remaining borders. Attach these border strips to the right and left of the swan block.

Repeat this process for the second swan block. Both swans will now have borders around three edges. Join the two blocks along the bottom edge so that the two swans are in mirror image.

Prepare a quilt sandwich of the quilt, wadding (batting) and backing (see General Techniques). Cut the backing fabric in half to create two pieces, each 58½in x width of fabric. Remove the selvedges and sew the two pieces together along the long edge using a ¼in seam allowance. Press the seam open. Trim the width down to 68in. Quilt as desired.

For a single-colour binding, cut six 2¼in x width of fabric strips and bind to finish (see General Techniques: Binding).

For a two-tone binding similar to my quilt, you will need three 2¼in x width of fabric strips of each colour. Sew the same colour strips together using diagonal seams. Sew the two colours together using a vertical seam and press the seam open. Align the waterline of the quilt with the vertical join in the binding strip (this will be the centre point of your binding). Start sewing from this central binding point in a clockwise direction and attach the binding to the quilt. Stop sewing approximately 4in from the waterline on the opposite side. Return to the centre point of the binding and attach the binding in an anti-clockwise direction. Do this very carefully, as you will be sewing in the 'wrong' direction with the bulk of the quilt squeezing through the neck of the sewing machine. Stop sewing approximately 4in from the waterline. Join the binding tails together as described in General Techniques: Binding (step 4).

QUILT ASSEMBLY DIAGRAM

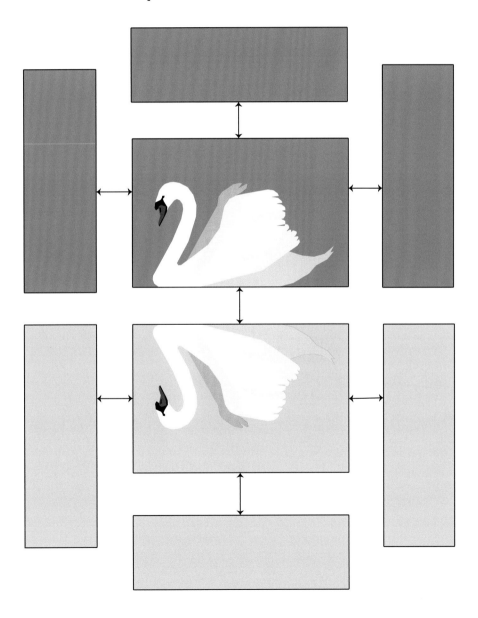

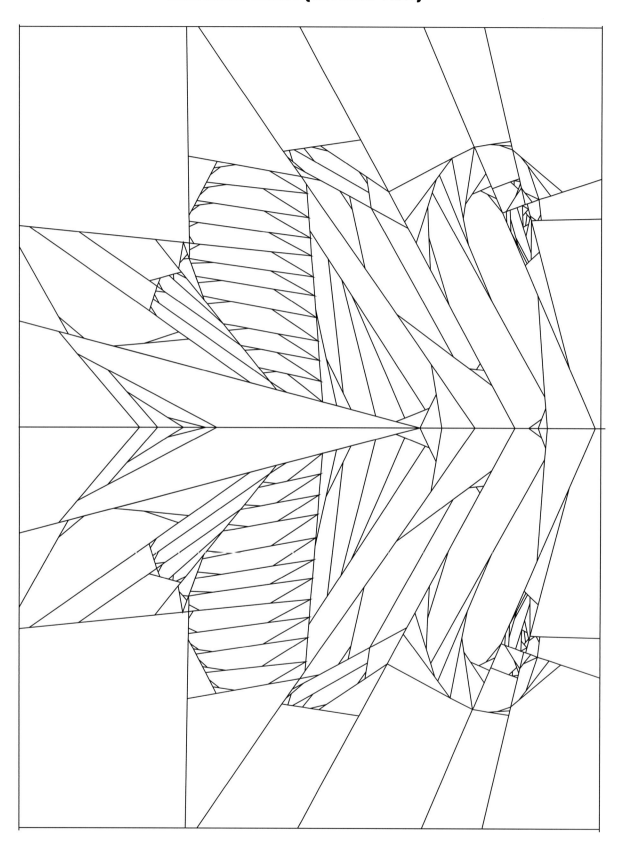

Potential Uses for this Block

WALL HANGING: If you were not keen to piece two swans, you could create a single swan. In this case, you may want to square up the block to create a 30in x 30in quilt. Do this by attaching 5½in borders to the top and bottom of the block. Perhaps you could make the bottom border a different colour, to mimic a waterline. For a single swan with border (30in x 30in) you will need: 1¼yds background, 1yd white low-volume tone-on-tone fabric, ⅛yd black, ⅛yd orange, ½yd border fabric, 38in x 38in backing fabric and wadding (batting), ¼yd binding fabric.

TABLE OR BED RUNNER: Instead of having reflected swans, you could sew a pair of swans facing each other. This would create a long, narrow quilt, which could be used for a table runner or bed runner. The fabric requirements would be the same as for the main quilt, but borders would not be required.

LARGE BED QUILT: Those who are up for a larger challenge and are feeling ambitious could create a pair of facing reflected swans. This would make a stunning quilt for a large bed. I suggest adding borders to ensure that the swans remain on the top of the bed while the borders provide the drape over the edge.

GENERAL TECHNIQUES

PRESSING

Pressing is very important when making blocks and assembling quilts. Remember, in quilt-making, you don't iron but 'press' to avoid distorting the fabric. Always set your seam after sewing by pressing the seam as sewn, to ease tension and prevent the seam line from distorting. Then open up the fabric pieces and press on the right side of the fabric, usually towards the darker fabric (or as described in the project). If necessary, guide the seam underneath to make sure the seam is going in the right direction. When pressing fabric pieces in foundation paper piecing it is often helpful to press seams open, to reduce bulk. Take care if using steam and don't use steam anywhere near a bias edge.

BORDERS

Some of the quilts in the book already have borders, but you can add a border to any of the designs to make them larger. When attaching a border it is important to do it properly, because a badly attached border will flare and never lie flat.

1 Start by measuring your trimmed quilt – see **Fig 1**. Measure the height along the left edge (a), along the right edge (b) and down the centre (c). Add the three measurements together and divide by three to give an average measurement (d). This is the length that the two side borders need to be cut.

2 To sew the side border strips in place, fold the quilt in half lengthwise. Place a pin on the fold to mark the centre point. Fold it in half again and place pins in the two resulting folds to mark the quarter points. Fold the two side border strips in the same way to mark the same points along the edge.

3 Pin the border to the body of the quilt with right sides together, ensuring that the ends line up and that all the pin-marked points are pinned to each other. Place a few more pins between these points, ensuring that the fabric is evenly distributed (**Fig 2**). Sew the border strips in place (**Fig 3**). You may need to ease the fabric slightly while sewing a border to the body of the quilt, but by using this method you will create a beautifully squared quilt. Press the border seams.

4 Use the same method to measure and attach the top and bottom border strips (**Fig 4**).

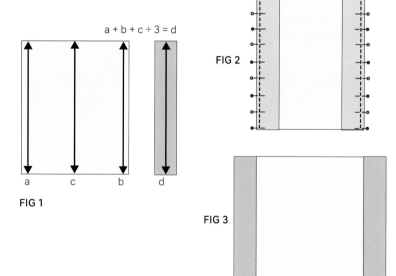

$a + b + c \div 3 = d$

a   c   b   d

FIG 1

FIG 2

FIG 3

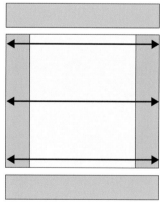

FIG 4

BACKING FABRIC

The fabric requirements for the backing fabric and the wadding (batting) in the larger projects are given with an extra 4in all round, to allow for long-arm quilting should you wish to use this service. For the smaller projects, or if you are quilting on a domestic machine at home (or by hand), then you will probably only need an extra 2in all round. So, remember that the backing will always need to be larger than the quilt top.

If the backing needed for a quilt is 42in or less on one side, then you can use a width-of-fabric piece. For example, if the quilt backing needs to be 42in x 72in, then buy 2yds of fabric. Trim off the selvedges so the width is 42in. The length will be as you bought it, i.e., 2yds (72in).

If your quilt is more than 42in on one side, then you will need to piece the backing (unless you plan to use extra-wide backing fabric). For example, the Howl quilt top is 60in x 80in. If you wanted to have the quilt long-arm quilted, you would need a backing piece measuring 68in x 88in (allowing 4in extra all round for the quilting process). A backing this size can be made up of two pieces each cut 34¼in x 88in and then sewn together along the long edge

to make a piece 68in wide x 88in long – see **Fig 5**. Two pieces 88in long need a total yardage of 4.8, i.e., 5yds of backing in total. Always press piecing seams on backing fabric open to reduce bulk.

MAKING A QUILT SANDWICH

Everyone has their favourite method of making a quilt sandwich – tacking (basting) or pins or spray glue – so use the method you are comfortable with. Place the pressed backing fabric right side down and smooth it flat. Add the wadding (batting) on top, wrinkle free, and then add the quilt right side up. Secure the layers well. If you are having the quilt long-arm quilted then you won't need to make a sandwich as the long-arm quilter will do that.

QUILTING

One of the fun things about quilting is that it can really emphasize the details of a design. The majority of the quilts in this book were custom quilted by Leeanne Hopper, a talented long-arm quilter. She

knows without asking that my preferred option is to stitch in the ditch around the important elements of the design and then use filler designs to fill the background and, where necessary, the animal. She always does an outstanding job for me, but I must admit that it is not necessary to pay to get the quilting done. I quilted Hunted myself. The majority of the work was done using a walking foot. I stitched in the ditch around the owl and many of the feathers, to emphasize the outline. If there were spots where I felt that the contrast between background and foreground was not as great as I would like it to be, then I used a contrasting thread to emphasize the fabric transition. The background was filled with gently waving parallel lines. I was a little bit adventurous and added free-motion quilting to the owl itself.

For those who feel that their quilting skills are not up to this level of detail, all is not lost. Great contemporary results can be achieved with simple straight-line quilting over the whole quilt.

When quilting, take care in areas where there are lots of small pieces as these can become bulky and may need you to work more slowly and cautiously than normal.

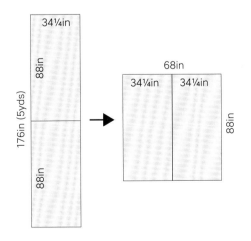

FIG 5

BINDING

The fabric requirements in this book are for a 2¼in double-fold binding cut on the straight grain.

1 Trim the excess backing and wadding (batting) so that the edges are even with the quilt top.

2 Join the binding strips together with 45-degree seams, as follows. Trim off selvedges. Lay two strips right sides together at right angles to each other. Sew diagonally from outside corner to outside corner. Trim to a ¼in seam and press the seam open. By joining the seams in this way, there is minimal bulk created in a single spot. The only time that I would join binding using a vertical seam is if I was using stripes or a print that will clearly show the join. When the binding strips are sewn into a continuous length, make sure there is sufficient to go around the quilt plus about 10in extra to allow for corners and overlapping ends. Aim to start roughly in the centre of one side, but before you start sewing, check to make sure that none of your binding joins fall on a corner, as this can create an ugly, bulky corner. If necessary, reposition your binding to avoid this.

3 With wrong sides together, press the binding in half lengthways. On the right side of the quilt and leaving a binding tail of about 5in, align the raw edges of the double thickness binding with the raw edge of the quilt and pin to hold in place. Sew with a ¼in seam allowance. At the first corner, stop ¼in from the edge of the fabric and backstitch (**Fig 6**). Lift the needle and presser foot (or take the quilt off the machine if you prefer) and fold the binding upwards (**Fig 7**). Fold the binding again but downwards (**Fig 8**). Stitch from the edge to ¼in from the next corner and repeat the turn. Continue all around the quilt working each corner in the same way.

4 When you return to the first side, leave a binding tail and an unsewn gap of about 8in. Lay both binding tails along the remaining unsewn edge. At a point in the centre of the stitching gap, fold the binding pieces back on themselves – the folds of the two ends should butt against each other. Press these folds to create clear creases. Now unfold the binding and lay the tails with right sides together at right angles to each other. Line up the crosses formed by the central fold of the binding and the fold that you just created. At this point, I like to place two pins on the diagonal (to check that I am about to sew the correct diagonal). Sew the seam, trim to a ¼in seam allowance and press the seam open. Now sew the remaining section of the binding in place on the quilt.

5 Press the binding away from the front of the quilt. Fold the binding over to the back of the quilt and hand stitch in place, folding the binding at each corner to form a neat mitre.

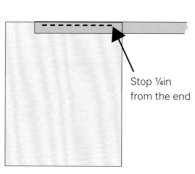

Stop ¼in from the end

FIG 6

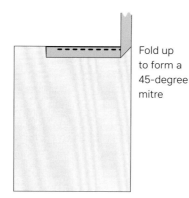

Fold up to form a 45-degree mitre

FIG 7

Fold down and stitch from the edge to a ¼in from the next corner

FIG 8

MAKING A CUSHION COVER

I tend to sew zips into my cushions, which you can do too if you like. However, you might prefer a simple Oxford-style cushion cover, which is quick and easy. This method doesn't usually have any fastenings but just a hemmed opening that overlaps at the centre.

1 Start by calculating the size of the two backing pieces needed, as follows. Measure the width of the cushion, divide this number in half and then add 4in. So, for a 20in wide cushion, this would be 20in ÷ 2 = 10in + 4in = 14in. Cut two pieces this width. The height of the pieces needs to be the same as the front of the cushion.

2 On both pieces of fabric along one long side, create a hem by turning the edge over by about ½in, twice. Sew with matching thread and press (**Fig 9**).

3 Place the patchwork cushion front right side up. Place one backing piece on top, right side down and with the hem towards the centre. Place the second backing piece on top, right side down and with the hem towards the centre. Make sure the outer edges of all three pieces are aligned and pin in place (**Fig 10**).

4 Sew the layers together around the outside, using a ¼in–⅜in seam. Remove pins, clip the corners a little to remove bulk and press. Turn through to the right side. Poke out the corners well and press. Insert a cushion pad to finish.

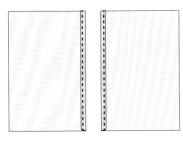

FIG 9

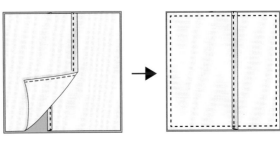

FIG 10

ACKNOWLEDGMENTS

I would like to extend a huge thank you to the entire publishing team and especially Sarah Callard for taking a chance on this New Zealand-based girl. It has been a real pleasure working with Jeni Hennah, Anna Wade and the team behind the scenes. My editor Lin Clements kept me in line and stopped me from over-thinking things. I really appreciated your help and guidance.

Leeanne Hopper of Quiltmekiwi is the genius long-arm quilter who worked magic on my quilts. She is always a pleasure to work with and never disappoints.

The inspiration for the barn owl in my Hunted quilt came from a photograph taken by Graham Jones called 'Flight of the Barn Owl'. He generously gave permission for me to base my quilt on his image.

I would like to thank Moda Fabrics for providing fabrics for the Monarch Butterfly quilt, Free Spirit for providing the Kaffe Fassett fabrics used in the Peacock, Rhino and Clydesdale Horse quilts and Oakshott Fabrics for providing the beautiful shot cottons used in Howl.

Writing this book has taken a lot of my time and energy. Without the love and understanding of my family it would not have been possible. Frank stepped up and took on the mammoth share of the housework so that I could concentrate on all things quilty. Keira and Stuart are my number one fans and can always be relied upon to provide inspiration and considered feedback.

Finally, a huge thank you must go to my friend Deb Robertson, who has always had absolute faith in my quilting abilities and predicted that I would write a quilting book about two years before I even contemplated it.

ABOUT THE AUTHOR

Juliet discovered foundation paper piecing when her two children were babies. In days filled with nappies, feeding and negotiating with small children it gave her joy to achieve something creative. Juliet's pre-child life included careers in archaeology and radiography. These two seemingly disparate careers, taught Juliet to pay attention to details and be logical in her approach. They also encouraged her to analyze how shapes and objects are constructed. These skills give the unique perspective that make her patterns so special. Originally from Scotland, Juliet and her husband live in a village in New Zealand and enjoy family hikes in the hills, watching their kids play Saturday rugby, and having a quiet coffee at the local cafe. These days Juliet spends her days designing paper-pieced patterns, which she sells under the name The Tartankiwi. For links to shops supplying Juliet's patterns, go to Juliet's blog: www.thetartankiwi.com

SUPPLIERS

UK

Bramble Patch

West Street, Weedon, Northampton, NN7 4QU

tel: 01327 342212

www.bramblepatchonline.com

The Cotton Patch

1283–1285 Stratford Rd, Birmingham, B28 9AJ

tel: 0121 702 2840

www.cottonpatch.co.uk

Eternal Maker

41 Terminus Rd, Chichester, PO19 8TX

tel: 01243 788174

www.eternalmaker.com

My Bearpaw

50 Lochrin Buildings, Gilmore Place, Edinburgh, Midlothian, EH3 9ND

tel: 0131 228 6377

www.mybearpaw.com

Oakshott Fabrics

19 Bamel Way, Brockworth, Gloucester, GL3 4BH

tel: 07486 463821

www.oakshottfabrics.com

The Add-A-Quarter™ ruler can be obtained from many online suppliers, so search for the product using a search engine.

USA

Fat Quarter Shop

2899 Business Park Drive, Buda, TX 78610

www.fatquartershop.com

Hawthorne Supply Co

54 Elizabeth Street, Suite 34, Red Hook, NY 12571

www.hawthornesupplyco.com

Pink Castle Fabrics

1915 Federal Blvd, Ann Arbor, MI 48103

www.pinkcastlefabrics.com

Stash Fabrics

395 Winkler Dr. Ste 200, Alpharetta, GA 30004

www.stashfabrics.com

New Zealand

Bolt of Cloth

The Tannery, 3 Garlands Road, Woolston, Christchurch

www.boltofcloth.com

Cushlas Village Fabrics

38 Victoria Rd, Devonport

136 Aranui Rd, Mapua, Nelson

www.cushlasvillagefabrics.co.nz

Donna's Quilt Studio

27a Corrin Street, Melville, Hamilton

www.donnasquiltstudio.co.nz

Juliet van der Heijden

For information on Juliet's patterns and tutorials

www.thetartankiwi.com

Stitchbird Fabrics

Shop 25 Kilbirnie Plaza, 22 Bay Rd, Kilbirnie, Wellington

www.stitchbird.co.nz

INDEX

A DAVID AND CHARLES BOOK
© David and Charles, Ltd 2017

David and Charles is an imprint of David and Charles, Ltd
1 Emperor Way, Exeter Business Park, Exeter, EX1 3QS

Text and Designs © Juliet van der Heijden 2017
Layout and Photography © David and Charles, Ltd 2017

First published in the UK and USA in 2017

A catalogue record for this book is available from the British Library.

ISBN-13: 978-1-4463-0667-3 paperback

ISBN-13: 978-1-4463-7634-8 EPUB

Printed in UK by Pureprint for:
David and Charles, Ltd
1 Emperor Way, Exeter Business Park, Exeter, EX1 3QS

10 9 8 7 6 5 4 3

Content Director: Ame Verso
Acquisitions Editor: Sarah Callard
Senior Editor: Jeni Hennah
Project Editor: Lin Clements
Proofreader: Cheryl Brown
Design Manager: Anna Wade
Designers: Lorraine Inglis and Sam Staddon
Art Direction: Sarah Rowntree
Photographer: Jason Jenkins
Production Manager: Beverley Richardson

David and Charles publishes high-quality books on a wide range of subjects. For more information visit www.davidandcharles.com.

Layout of the digital edition of this book may vary depending on reader hardware and display settings.